AI OPERATING SYSTEMS

H. Peter Alesso

Also by H. Peter Alesso

AI Langlands Program
AI HIVE © 2025.
Tomorrow's Film Studio Today
Video Software Lab © 2025.
Absolute Zero Reasoner
AI HIVE © 2025.
Vibe Coding by Example
AI HIVE © 2025.
Connections: Patterns of Discovery,
John Wiley & Sons, © 2008.
Thinking on the Web,
John Wiley & Sons, Inc., © 2006,
Developing Semantic Web Services,
A. K. Peters, Ltd., © 2004,
Building the Intelligent Wireless Web,
Addison Wesley, © 2002,
e-Video: Producing Internet Video as Broadband Technologies Converge,
Addison-Wesley, © 2000,

AI OPERATING SYSTEMS

H. Peter Alesso © 2025
hpeteralesso.com

AI HIVE Publications

Pleasanton, CA 94566

Edition 1.00

SYNOPSIS

*How Artificial Intelligence
Redefines Computing*

For forty years, we've used operating systems designed for a world that no longer exists. We still click through folders and menus conceived when computers filled entire rooms, while our smartphones surpassed yesterday's supercomputers. A revolution is underway that will transform not just how we use computers, but what computers fundamentally are.

AI Operating System reveals computing's next great leap: from machines that follow instructions to systems that understand intentions. The book traces three eras of software evolution—from explicit programming (Software 1.0) through machine learning (Software 2.0) to our current threshold of natural language computing (Software 3.0), where AI becomes the computational foundation itself. Recent standards like Anthropic's Model Context Protocol (MCP) exemplify this shift, providing standardized connections for LLMs to external tools and data, as detailed in Chapter 6 on "The LLM as a Computing Platform."

Today's operating systems, masterpieces of Software 1.0, are increasingly mismatched with modern needs. They react rather than anticipate, fragment rather than integrate. We search for files whose names we've forgotten, watch powerful computers inexplicably slow down, and manually shuttle data between applications. These aren't random frustrations—they're symptoms of architectural limits.

The tech giants see this. Microsoft's Copilot, Apple's Neural Engine, and Google's Fuchsia represent ambitious attempts to add AI to existing systems. But these efforts reveal a deeper truth: retrofitting intelligence onto traditional architectures is like attaching wings to a car. We need to rebuild from the ground up.

The book explores the technologies making AI-native operating systems possible. Microkernel architectures provide security and modularity for AI workloads. Neural processing units and confidential computing enable efficient, private AI computation. Large language models emerge not as applications but as computational platforms. Combined, these enable systems that are intelligent by design.

Imagine computers that understand context and anticipate needs—preparing resources before you need them, organizing information by meaning, not file names, and enabling natural conversation instead of clicking through menus. Privacy is guaranteed by hardware. Applications are dissolving into capabilities that flow together seamlessly.

AI Operating System is essential reading for software engineers, technology leaders, and anyone who wants to understand the future of computing. Through accessible explanations and vivid examples, it reveals how AI will transform the most fundamental layer of our digital world. The question isn't whether this transformation will happen, but whether we're ready for it. Example LLM-OS provided: https://github.com/alessoh/llm-os Grace Hopper's moth gave us the term "computer bug" and symbolized the concept of deterministic computing. The AI revolution promises something profound: computers that understand the intentions behind the instructions.

CONTENTS

Chapter 1: Three Eras of Software
Chapter 2: The Current Operating System Landscape
Chapter 3: Early AI Integration Attempts
Chapter 4: Microkernel Architectures for AI
Chapter 5: Hardware Foundations
Chapter 6: The LLM as a Computing Platform
Chapter 7: Conversational Interfaces
Chapter 8: Proactive Resource Management
Chapter 9: Intelligent File Systems
Chapter 10: Security in the AI Era
Chapter 11: Enterprise AI Platforms
Chapter 12: Edge and IoT Integration
Chapter 13: Privacy and Trust
Chapter 14: Reimagining Productivity
Chapter 15: Personalization and Adaptation
Chapter 16: Collaborative Intelligence
Chapter 17: Technical Challenges
Chapter 18: Social and Ethical Implication
Chapter 19: Transition Period
Chapter 20: Next Decade
Glossary
References

CHAPTER 1

Eras of Software

Grace Hopper was debugging the Harvard Mark II computer in 1947 when she found it—a moth trapped in a relay, the first literal computer bug. She taped it into the logbook with the notation "First actual case of bug being found." In that moment, she was working in what we now recognize as the dawn of Software 1.0, an era that would dominate computing for the next six decades.

Back then, every instruction had to be explicitly written. Every behavior had to be programmed. Every edge case had to be anticipated. The contract between human and machine was simple: perfect clarity in exchange for perfect obedience. Whether you were punching cards in the 1950s or writing Python scripts in the 2000s, the fundamental relationship remained unchanged. Humans wrote precise instructions, and computers followed them exactly.

This deterministic world gave us the operating

systems we still use today. UNIX, Windows, macOS—they're all masterpieces of Software 1.0 thinking. They manage resources through carefully crafted algorithms, schedule processes through explicit rules, and provide abstractions so reliable they've become invisible. When you save a file, you trust it will be there when you return. When you click an icon, you know what will happen. This predictability became the foundation of the entire digital age.

But Software 1.0 had a fundamental limitation. It could only do what programmers explicitly told it to do. It couldn't learn from experience. It couldn't adapt to new situations. It couldn't handle problems its creators hadn't anticipated. For tasks like recognizing faces in photos or understanding human speech, traditional programming hit a wall. You simply couldn't write enough if-then statements to capture the messy complexity of the real world.

Everything changed in 2012. That year, a neural network called AlexNet achieved breakthrough performance in image recognition, not through clever algorithms or hand-crafted features, but by learning. Instead of programmers writing rules to identify cats in photos, AlexNet learned to recognize them by adjusting millions of numerical weights. This was Software 2.0—programs written not in code, but in numbers.

The implications rippled through the technology world. Suddenly, computers could do things that had seemed impossible just years before. They could transcribe speech, translate languages, and even beat world champions at Go. Instead of writing explicit rules, developers were now crafting neural architectures and curating datasets. The "program" had become a matrix of floating-point numbers that somehow encoded learned behaviors.

Operating systems began incorporating these capabilities, but only at the edges. Your phone might use a neural network to recognize your face, or your computer might use one to enhance your photos. But at their core, operating systems remained firmly rooted in Software 1.0 principles. The neural networks were powerful tools, but they were still just passengers in a system designed for explicit code.

Then came the large language models, and with them, Software 3.0. When OpenAI released GPT-3 in 2020, something fundamental shifted. Here was a system that could understand and generate human language with unprecedented sophistication. More remarkably, it could follow complex instructions, reason through problems, and even write code—all through the medium of natural conversation.

The progression was striking. In Software 1.0, we told computers exactly what to do. In Software 2.0, we showed them examples and let them learn patterns. In Software 3.0, we simply explain what we want in plain language, and the system figures out how to do it. The prompt has become the new programming language, but unlike traditional programming languages with their rigid syntax, prompts are expressed in the fluid, contextual medium of human language.

This shift is revolutionary because it democratizes computing in a way nothing before has achieved. You no longer need to learn Python or C++ to make computers do complex tasks. You need only explain what you want, as you might to a knowledgeable colleague. The large language model serves as a universal translator between human intent and computational capability.

But perhaps the most profound change is the move from deterministic to probabilistic computing. Software 1.0 was built on certainty—run the same program twice, get the same result. Software 2.0 introduced uncertainty at the edges—a neural network might be 98% confident about its answer. Software 3.0 embraces uncertainty at its core. When an LLM generates text, it's sampling from probability distributions, making countless tiny decisions about what word should come next.

This probabilistic nature isn't a weakness to be overcome; it's what enables these systems to handle the ambiguity and complexity of the real world. They can work with incomplete information, generate creative solutions, and adapt to context in ways deterministic systems never could. But it also challenges our fundamental assumptions about what computers are and how they should behave.

Standing at this transition point, we can see that these three eras of software demand three different kinds of operating systems. The operating systems we use today—Windows, macOS, Linux—are brilliant expressions of Software 1.0 thinking. They're deterministic, predictable, and built on decades of refined abstractions. But they're increasingly mismatched with a world moving toward Software 3.0.

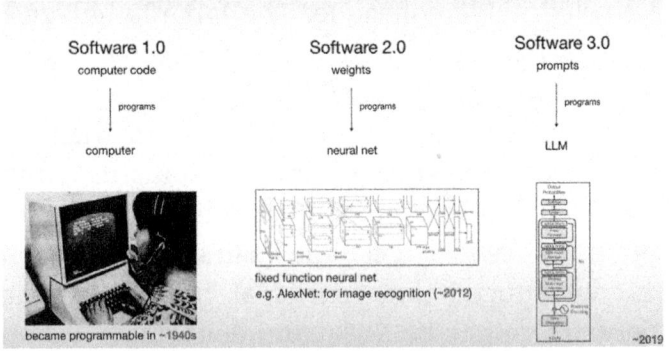

Figure 1 Software Eras

What would an operating system look like if it were built from the ground up for Software 3.0? What if natural language were the primary interface? What if learning and adaptation were core capabilities rather than add-on features? What if the boundary between user and system became a fluid collaboration rather than a rigid interface?

These aren't just theoretical questions. As we'll see in the chapters ahead, the answers are beginning to take shape. The moth Grace Hopper found gave us the term "computer bug" and symbolized an era of explicit, deterministic computing. The AI revolution promises something far more profound: computers that understand not just our instructions, but our intentions. The question isn't whether this transformation will happen, but how quickly we can adapt to a world where it has.

CHAPTER 2

Current OS Landscape

Every morning, millions of us perform the same ritual. We open our laptops or unlock our phones, click through familiar interfaces, and navigate digital worlds that have only marginally changed in decades. The irony is striking: we're using interfaces designed in the 1970s and 80s to manage technologies and workflows that would have been pure science fiction to their creators.

Think about your last frustrating computer experience. Maybe you were searching for a file whose name you'd forgotten, clicking through endless folders like a digital archaeologist. Perhaps your computer slowed to a crawl while rendering a video, even though you have a machine thousands of times more powerful than the computers that sent humans to the moon. Or maybe you found yourself copying and pasting between a dozen applications, manually stitching together information that should flow seamlessly.

These frustrations aren't random glitches or user errors. They're symptoms of a deeper mismatch between how our operating systems work and how we actually use computers today. To understand why AI-native operating systems are inevitable, we first need to understand the elegant prison we've built for ourselves.

At the heart of every operating system lies the kernel, a piece of software so fundamental that most users never think about it. The kernel is like the conductor of an vast orchestra, coordinating thousands of simultaneous performances. When you type a letter, the kernel ensures it appears on screen. When you save a file, the kernel finds space on your disk and remembers where it put it. When you run multiple programs, the kernel switches between them thousands of times per second, creating the illusion they're all running at once.

This architecture was revolutionary when it was invented. The ability to run multiple programs simultaneously, to abstract away hardware differences, to provide security and stability—these were breakthrough innovations that enabled the personal computer revolution. But they were designed for a world that no longer exists.

Consider how your operating system manages resources. When you launch Photoshop, the OS doesn't know you're about to open a massive image file. It reacts to each request as it comes, allocating memory bit by bit, ramping up CPU usage as needed. It's always playing catch-up, like a waiter who only starts cooking when customers arrive at the restaurant. This reactive approach made sense when computers were simpler and workloads were predictable. But modern computing is neither simple nor predictable.

The problem becomes acute with today's workloads. When a data scientist starts training a machine learning model, the resource requirements are largely predictable—the OS could prepare memory, optimize CPU and GPU coordination, and adjust system priorities in advance. But it doesn't. It waits and reacts, leading to the familiar experience of a system that feels sluggish despite having tremendous computational power.

This reactive nature extends beyond resource management to the entire way we interact with computers. The operating system doesn't learn that you always open certain applications together. It doesn't notice that you regularly perform the same sequence of actions every Monday morning. It doesn't adapt its behavior based on your patterns. Every day is Groundhog Day for your OS—it has no memory of what you did yesterday or what you're likely to do tomorrow.

The way applications talk to the operating system and each other reveals another fundamental limitation. These conversations happen through Application Programming Interfaces—APIs—that are like diplomatic protocols between nations. They're formal, rigid, and slow to change. When a program wants to save a file, it must speak the precise language the operating system expects. When two programs need to share data, they must find a common format and often resort to the digital equivalent of passing notes—copying and pasting through the clipboard.

This rigid communication creates absurd situations. You might have a photo in one application and want to edit it in another. Despite both programs understanding images, you often need to save the file from one, navigate the file system to find it, then open it in the other. It's like two people who speak the same language being forced to communicate through written letters instead of talking directly.

The API paradigm also creates a massive semantic gap. There's often a chasm between what you want to accomplish and the tools available. Want to "find all photos from last summer's vacation"? This simple human request might require navigating multiple applications, remembering file naming conventions, checking various cloud services, and manually sorting through results. The computer has all the information needed to answer your question, but the rigid APIs make it nearly impossible to ask it directly.

These interfaces we use daily—whether graphical or command-line—are showing their age even more starkly. The desktop metaphor made perfect sense when people were transitioning from physical offices to digital ones. Files and folders were brilliant abstractions for documents and filing cabinets. But we're now trying to manage millions of files, thousands of applications, and endless streams of information using metaphors designed for a few dozen documents.

The command line, beloved by programmers and power users, demands perfect recall of arcane syntax. Quick: what's the difference between 'rm -rf' and 'rm -Rf'? Why is it 'ls' to list files but 'dir' on Windows? These interfaces are powerful but unforgiving, like ancient incantations that must be recited perfectly to work.

Even our modern attempts at improvement feel like bandages on a broken system. Voice assistants can set timers and play music but struggle with anything complex. Search functions can find files by name but not by meaning or context. Notification systems interrupt us constantly because they can't understand the difference between urgent and trivial.

The security model of current operating systems adds another layer of frustration. Designed for an era of isolated computers or small, trusted networks, it struggles with our always-connected, cloud-integrated world. The result is a constant barrage of permission dialogs that train users to click "Allow" without thinking, security warnings that cry wolf, and a system that can't meaningfully distinguish between legitimate software and threats.

We've tried to patch these problems with incremental improvements. Modern operating systems have search functions, but they're bolted on rather than fundamental. They have voice assistants, but they're limited to simple commands. They have security sandboxing, but it often breaks functionality users need. Each solution adds complexity without addressing the underlying architectural mismatches.

The tragedy is that our computers are more powerful than ever, yet they often feel slower and more frustrating than machines from decades ago. We have processors with dozens of cores, graphics cards that can render photorealistic worlds in real-time, and memory measured in gigabytes, yet we still see spinning beachballs and "Application Not Responding" messages. The raw power is there, but the operating system can't effectively harness it.

This isn't a failure of engineering—the engineers who build operating systems are brilliant. It's a failure of evolution. We've reached the limits of what can be achieved by incrementally improving designs from the 1960s and 70s. It's like trying to turn a steam engine into a jet engine by adding better pistons. At some point, you need to acknowledge that the fundamental architecture is the limitation.

Today's users don't think in terms of files and applications. They think in terms of projects, goals, and outcomes. A marketing manager doesn't want to "open PowerPoint, import Excel data, and search for images." They want to "create a presentation about last quarter's performance." The cognitive load of translating human intent into computer operations is a tax on productivity that we've accepted for so long we barely notice it anymore.

As we stand on the brink of the AI revolution, these limitations become even more apparent. We have systems that can understand natural language, learn from patterns, and even exhibit creativity. But we're trying to integrate them into operating systems that speak only in system calls and mouse clicks. It's not enough to add AI features to existing systems. We need operating systems built from the ground up for an AI-native world.

The next chapter explores how major technology companies have attempted to bridge this gap, adding AI capabilities to their existing operating systems. These efforts, while impressive, ultimately demonstrate why addition isn't enough. The future demands not evolution, but revolution—not better steam engines, but entirely new ways of thinking about what an operating system can be.

CHAPTER 3

Early AI Integration

The executives at Microsoft, Apple, and Google could see the writing on the wall. AI wasn't just another technology trend—it was a fundamental shift in computing. Each company, shaped by its own culture and constraints, began the delicate operation of grafting intelligence onto their existing operating systems. These attempts would prove both inspiring and revealing, showing us glimpses of the future while exposing the limitations of the present.

Microsoft moved first with characteristic boldness. The announcement of Copilot for Windows represented the company's biggest interface change since the introduction of the Start menu. Here was an AI assistant that lived in a sidebar, ready to help with everything from system settings to creative tasks. The demos were impressive: users could ask Copilot to summarize documents, adjust computer settings in natural language, or help write emails. It seemed like the natural evolution of the operating system—a knowledgeable assistant always at your side.

But as users began working with Copilot, the seams started showing. Ask it to "optimize my computer for video editing," and it might suggest closing some applications or tweaking a few settings. What it couldn't do was fundamentally reorganize how Windows allocates resources. It couldn't predictively load video editing tools into memory before you needed them. It couldn't intelligently route processing tasks between CPU and GPU based on your specific workflow. Copilot was like a brilliant assistant working in an old office building—helpful and knowledgeable, but constrained by the infrastructure around it.

The architectural reality was stark. Windows carries decades of legacy code, millions of existing applications, and compatibility requirements stretching back to the 1990s. Copilot had to work within these constraints, becoming another layer in an already complex system rather than a fundamental rethinking of how the OS operates. It could help you find the right settings menu, but it couldn't eliminate the need for settings menus in the first place.

The integration also revealed a deeper philosophical challenge. Traditional operating systems are built on predictability and control. Users expect the same action to produce the same result every time. But AI systems are inherently probabilistic—they generate responses based on patterns and possibilities. Trying to merge these two paradigms within the existing Windows architecture was like trying to add jazz improvisation to a classical symphony orchestra. Both are beautiful, but they follow fundamentally different rules.

Apple, true to form, took a completely different approach. Rather than adding a visible AI layer, they went straight to the silicon. The Neural Engine, first appearing in the iPhone X's A11 Bionic chip, represented a bet that AI's future lay not in software additions but in hardware acceleration. This wasn't just a faster processor—it was specialized silicon designed specifically for the mathematical operations that power neural networks.

The results were immediately impressive. Face ID could recognize you in milliseconds. Photos could identify people, places, and objects without sending data to the cloud. Siri could process many requests entirely on-device. The Neural Engine could perform trillions of operations per second while sipping battery power. It was elegant, private, and powerful—everything Apple stands for.

Yet for all its sophistication, the Neural Engine revealed the limitations of hardware-first thinking. Having a Formula One engine doesn't help much if you're still driving on roads designed for horse-drawn carriages. Applications could use Core ML to run machine learning models efficiently, but they still communicated through traditional APIs. The file system still organized data in rigid hierarchies. The interface still required tapping, clicking, and swiping through predetermined paths.

The Neural Engine accelerated AI tasks brilliantly, but it didn't transform how users interact with their devices. You still had to remember which app to open for which task. You still had to navigate through menus and settings. You still had to manually move information between applications. It was like having a supercomputer that you could only communicate with through a telegraph.

More telling was what Apple didn't do with this powerful hardware. Despite having neural processing capabilities in every device, iOS and macOS remained fundamentally traditional in their architecture. The OS didn't learn your patterns over time. It didn't adapt its interface based on your usage. It didn't enable applications to share intelligence or context. The Neural Engine was a powerful tool trapped in a conventional toolbox.

While Microsoft and Apple were retrofitting their existing systems, Google pursued a more radical path with Fuchsia. Started in 2016, Fuchsia represented something almost unheard of in the operating system world: a complete do-over. Free from the constraints of Linux (which powers Android and Chrome OS), Google's engineers could design a modern OS from scratch.

The technical details were impressive. Fuchsia used a microkernel architecture called Zircon, designed for security and modularity. Instead of traditional file permissions, it used capability-based security—a more flexible and powerful model that could theoretically enable AI-driven access control. The entire system was built with modern programming languages and contemporary software engineering practices.

Google deployed Fuchsia quietly, first appearing in some Nest smart home devices. This wasn't the splashy consumer launch of a new OS—it was a careful, methodical testing of new ideas in controlled environments. The choice of IoT devices was strategic. These environments demanded real-time performance and efficient resource usage while running AI workloads at the edge. If Fuchsia could succeed here, it might point the way toward a broader transformation.

But even Fuchsia, for all its modern architecture, hadn't made the full leap to AI-native design. It provided a cleaner foundation than traditional operating systems, but it still maintained conventional abstractions. Programs were still programs. Files were still files. The interface between human and machine remained mediated by traditional paradigms. Fuchsia was like a state-of-the-art building constructed with future expansion in mind, but still fundamentally designed for current ways of working.

These three approaches—Microsoft's overlay strategy, Apple's hardware acceleration, and Google's clean-slate architecture—taught the industry valuable lessons. Each company had pushed the boundaries in their own way, and each had hit similar walls.

The most fundamental limitation was what we might call the "integration paradox." The more successfully AI was added to existing systems, the more apparent it became that addition wasn't enough. It was like adding wings to a car—you might achieve brief moments of flight, but you're still fundamentally driving a car, not piloting an aircraft.

Consider the workflow gaps that persisted despite these innovations. When you switched between applications, AI assistants lost all context. Copilot didn't know what you were doing in Adobe Premiere. Siri couldn't understand the relationship between your email draft and your calendar appointment. Each AI interaction started fresh, like a helpful stranger with no memory of your previous conversations.

The semantic blindness was equally frustrating. These systems could process natural language commands but couldn't understand the deeper relationships between your data. They could find a file named "Q3_Report.pdf" but couldn't identify all documents related to third-quarter performance across different applications and formats. They could set a reminder but couldn't understand how it related to your project deadlines.

Perhaps most limiting was the persistent reactive nature of these systems. Even with AI integration, they waited for commands rather than anticipating needs. They couldn't prepare resources based on learned patterns. They couldn't optimize for upcoming tasks. They remained fundamentally responsive rather than proactive, like a assistant who waits to be asked rather than anticipating what you need.

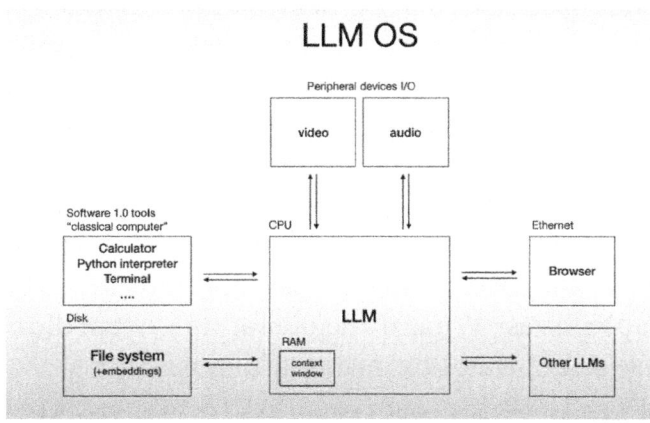

Figure 2 LLM OS (Andrej Karpathy © 2023**)**

These early attempts weren't failures—they were necessary experiments that revealed the shape of the problem. Microsoft showed us the value of conversational interfaces while demonstrating their limitations when layered onto traditional systems. Apple proved that on-device AI processing was both feasible and desirable, but needed deeper architectural integration. Google demonstrated that modern architectures could provide better foundations for AI, but architecture alone wasn't enough.

The gap between what these companies achieved and what users actually needed wasn't just technical—it was conceptual. They were trying to add intelligence to operating systems, when what we really need are operating systems that are themselves intelligent. It's the difference between a building with smart features and a building that's genuinely intelligent about how it serves its occupants.

As we watched these tech giants grapple with AI integration, a new vision began to emerge. What if we stopped trying to add AI to existing systems and instead built systems around AI from the ground up? What if natural language wasn't just another input method but the primary interface? What if learning and adaptation weren't features but fundamental capabilities? What if the operating system didn't just use AI but was, in a meaningful sense, AI?

These questions would drive the next phase of innovation. The early attempts had shown us both the destination and the obstacles. Now it was time to chart an entirely new path—one that didn't just integrate AI into operating systems but reimagined what an operating system could be in an AI-native world. The journey from adding intelligence to becoming intelligent was about to become.

CHAPTER 4

Microkernel Architectures for AI

In a high-security facility in Sydney, Australia, a small team of researchers achieved something in 2009 that most thought impossible. They had formally verified seL4, a microkernel operating system—mathematically proving that its code did exactly what it was supposed to do, nothing more, nothing less. This wasn't just another academic exercise. It was a glimpse into a future where operating systems could be both powerful and provably secure, a combination that would prove essential for the AI revolution to come.

To understand why microkernels matter for AI, we need to first understand what makes them different. Traditional operating systems like Linux or Windows use what's called a monolithic kernel. Imagine a massive factory where everything happens under one roof—manufacturing, quality control, shipping, accounting, everything. It's efficient when things go well, but when something breaks, it can bring down the entire operation. A bug in a printer driver can crash your entire system. A misbehaving application can corrupt memory used by critical system functions.

Microkernels take a radically different approach. They reduce the kernel—the core of the operating system that runs with full system privileges—to the absolute minimum. In seL4, the entire kernel is less than 10,000 lines of code. To put that in perspective, the Linux kernel has over 30 million lines. Everything else—device drivers, file systems, even parts of memory management—runs as separate processes with limited privileges, like independent contractors rather than employees.

This architectural choice seemed almost quaint in an era of abundant computing power. Why add the overhead of all this separation when modern processors were so fast? Why complicate the system design when monolithic kernels had proven themselves over decades? The answer became clear only as we began to understand what AI-native operating systems would require.

The first insight came from security. AI systems, by their nature, handle vast amounts of sensitive data. They learn from user behavior, process personal information, and make decisions that affect everything from resource allocation to access control. In a traditional monolithic system, a compromise anywhere could potentially access everything. It's like having a master key that opens every door in a building—convenient for the owner, catastrophic if stolen.

Microkernels enforce what security researchers call the "principle of least privilege" at the most fundamental level. Each component gets exactly the permissions it needs, no more. The AI model processing your photos can't access your banking information. The natural language processor interpreting your commands can't directly modify system files. Even if an attacker compromises one component, they're trapped in a small box rather than having run of the entire system.

This isolation becomes even more critical when you consider how AI systems fail. Traditional software tends to fail in predictable ways—null pointer exceptions, buffer overflows, race conditions. These are bugs programmers can find and fix. But AI systems can fail in novel, unexpected ways. A neural network might produce bizarre outputs when given unusual inputs. A language model might hallucinate false information. A learning algorithm might develop unexpected biases.

In a monolithic system, these AI failures could cascade throughout the entire OS. Imagine an AI resource manager that develops a bias toward certain types of applications, gradually starving others of CPU time until the system becomes unusable. Or consider a natural language interface that misinterprets a command and begins deleting critical system files. These aren't theoretical concerns—they're the kinds of emergent behaviors that AI researchers observe regularly.

Microkernels contain these failures naturally. If an AI component misbehaves, it's isolated in its own process with limited capabilities. The system can detect the misbehavior, terminate the component, and restart it without affecting the rest of the system. It's like having circuit breakers throughout a building instead of one main fuse—a failure in one area doesn't plunge everything into darkness.

The modularity of microkernels offers another crucial advantage for AI systems: the ability to mix different types of computation safely. An AI-native operating system needs to run traditional deterministic code alongside probabilistic AI models. It needs to guarantee real-time performance for critical tasks while allowing AI components to take variable amounts of time. It needs to provide strong isolation between components that might not trust each other.

Consider a self-driving car running an AI-native operating system. The motor control systems need hard real-time guarantees—when the AI decides to brake, the brakes must engage within milliseconds. The vision processing system running neural networks might take variable time depending on scene complexity. The route planning system might spin up large language models to interpret natural language destinations. In a monolithic system, these different components with vastly different requirements would interfere with each other. In a microkernel, they run in isolation, each with appropriate scheduling and resource guarantees.

The formal verification of seL4 adds another layer of assurance. When mathematicians proved that seL4's implementation matches its specification, they created something unprecedented: an operating system kernel with no bugs in its core functionality. This doesn't mean the entire system is bug-free—the components running on top can still have issues. But it does mean the foundation is solid, like building on bedrock rather than sand.

This mathematical certainty becomes invaluable when building AI systems that need to be trustworthy. How can we trust an AI to manage critical infrastructure if we can't even trust the operating system it runs on? How can we build AI systems for healthcare, finance, or aviation without a provably correct foundation? The formal verification of microkernels provides that foundation.

The L4Re framework, built on the L4 microkernel family, shows how these principles scale to real-world systems. Used in everything from automotive systems to telecommunications infrastructure, L4Re demonstrates that microkernel-based systems can handle production workloads. It provides a framework for building complex systems from isolated components, each potentially running different operating system personalities or AI models.

But perhaps the most intriguing aspect of microkernels for AI is their potential for evolution.

In a monolithic system, changing core functionality requires modifying the kernel—a risky operation that affects everything. In a microkernel system, you can swap out components like replacing parts in a machine. Want to try a new AI scheduler? Deploy it as a separate process. Want to experiment with a novel memory management approach for neural networks? Run it alongside the existing system.

This evolutionary capability matters because we don't yet know the optimal architecture for AI-native operating systems. We're still discovering how best to integrate traditional and AI computation, how to manage resources for mixed workloads, how to provide interfaces that are both powerful and safe. Microkernels let us experiment with different approaches without committing to a single design.

The isolation also enables an intriguing possibility: heterogeneous trust. Not all AI models are created equal. Some are thoroughly tested and trusted. Others are experimental or come from third parties. In a microkernel system, you can run trusted AI components with more privileges while sandboxing experimental ones. You can let a verified AI model manage critical resources while restricting an untrusted one to advisory roles.

The performance overhead of microkernels, once seen as their fatal flaw, becomes less relevant in an AI context. The computation cost of message passing between isolated components pales in comparison to the cost of running neural network inference. The overhead of context switches becomes negligible when your AI models are performing billions of operations. And the benefits—security, reliability, modularity—become invaluable when building systems that learn and adapt.

As we stand on the brink of AI-native operating systems, microkernels offer something essential: a way to build systems that are both intelligent and trustworthy. They provide the isolation needed to contain AI failures, the modularity needed to evolve rapidly, and the security needed to handle sensitive data. They're not just a better architecture for AI—they're an enabling architecture that makes AI-native operating systems possible.

The researchers who verified seL4 probably didn't imagine their work would become crucial for AI systems. They were focused on building provably correct software for critical applications. But in doing so, they created a foundation for something larger: operating systems that can safely harness the power of AI while protecting us from its risks. As we'll see in the next chapter, this software foundation needs equally sophisticated hardware to reach its full potential. The marriage of microkernel architectures and AI-specific hardware will enable capabilities we're only beginning to imagine.

CHAPTER 5

Hardware Foundations

The chip designers at Apple faced a dilemma in 2016. They were developing the A11 Bionic processor for the next iPhone, and the requirements seemed impossible to reconcile. Face ID needed to process neural networks fast enough to unlock your phone without noticeable delay. Camera features demanded real-time AI processing for portraits and augmented reality. Battery life couldn't suffer. And all of this had to fit in a chip small enough for a phone that would slip into your pocket.

Their solution would reshape how we think about computer architecture. Instead of trying to make the CPU or GPU handle AI workloads—like forcing a concert pianist to play drums—they created something new: the Neural Engine. This wasn't just another accelerator. It was recognition that AI computation is fundamentally different from traditional processing, and it deserves its own place in silicon.

To understand why neural processing units represent such a breakthrough, consider what happens when a traditional CPU tries to run a neural network. Modern AI models consist of millions or billions of simple mathematical operations—multiplying numbers, adding them up, applying simple functions. A CPU, designed for complex, branching logic, tackles these operations one by one, like a master chef forced to work in a fast-food restaurant. It can do the job, but it's wastefully overqualified.

GPUs offered a better match. Originally designed for graphics, they excel at parallel operations—doing thousands of simple calculations simultaneously. This made them natural candidates for AI workloads. But GPUs are power-hungry beasts, designed for desktop computers with dedicated power supplies and cooling systems. Putting a traditional GPU in a phone would drain the battery in minutes and turn the device into a pocket warmer.

Neural processing units take a different approach. They're designed from the ground up for the specific mathematical operations that neural networks require. Where a CPU might take dozens of clock cycles to perform a matrix multiplication, an NPU does it in one. Where a GPU might waste energy on features neural networks don't need, an NPU includes only what's necessary. It's like the difference between a Swiss Army knife and a surgical scalpel—both are tools, but one is precisely designed for its specific task.

The numbers tell the story. Apple's Neural Engine can perform over 15 trillion operations per second while consuming just a few watts of power. To match that performance, a traditional CPU would need hundreds of watts—more power than most laptops use for their entire system. This isn't just an incremental improvement; it's a fundamental shift in what's possible.

But NPUs aren't just about raw performance. They enable a new model of computing where AI inference happens continuously in the background. Your phone can process every photo as you take it, enhance audio in real-time during calls, and predict what app you're likely to open next—all without draining the battery or making the device uncomfortably warm. It's ambient intelligence, always available but never intrusive.

This shift in hardware capabilities demands equally sophisticated security measures, which brings us to one of the most important but least visible innovations in modern processors: confidential computing. Intel's TDX (Trust Domain Extensions) and AMD's SEV-SNP (Secure Encrypted Virtualization-Secure Nested Paging) represent attempts to solve a fundamental problem: how can we run AI workloads on sensitive data without exposing that data to the system running the computation?

The problem is particularly acute for AI systems. Traditional software might need to process your credit card number briefly during a transaction.

AI systems need to learn from patterns in vast amounts of personal data—your photos, messages, health records, financial transactions. In current architectures, this data is vulnerable while being processed. It's encrypted on disk, encrypted in transit, but naked and exposed in memory during computation.

Confidential computing changes this equation. These technologies create secure enclaves—regions of memory that are encrypted even during processing. The CPU decrypts data only inside the processor itself, performs computations, and re-encrypts results before they leave. Even if an attacker has complete control of the operating system, they can't access data inside these enclaves. It's like having a sealed room inside a building where sensitive work can happen without fear of surveillance.

For AI-native operating systems, this capability is transformative. Imagine an AI assistant that learns from your behavior to provide better recommendations. With confidential computing, this learning can happen without exposing your raw data to the AI system itself. The model trains on encrypted data, producing encrypted updates that only you can decrypt. It's privacy-preserving AI at the hardware level.

The implications extend beyond personal privacy. Hospitals could collaborate on AI models for disease diagnosis without sharing patient data. Financial institutions could jointly train fraud detection systems without exposing customer transactions. Companies could benefit from collective AI intelligence without sacrificing competitive advantages. The hardware makes possible what policy and goodwill alone could never achieve.

But having powerful NPUs and secure enclaves isn't enough if the operating system can't orchestrate them effectively. This is where GPU-aware scheduling becomes crucial. Traditional schedulers treat all processors as interchangeable workers. They might send an AI workload to a busy GPU while an NPU sits idle, or worse, try to run neural network inference on a CPU while specialized hardware goes unused.

Modern schedulers need to understand the heterogeneous nature of AI workloads. Some operations run best on NPUs—the regular, predictable computations of neural network inference. Others need the flexibility of GPUs—training new models or running irregular algorithms. Still others require the CPU's ability to handle complex control flow. The scheduler becomes like a conductor who knows not just the music but the strengths of each instrument in the orchestra.

Kubernetes, the container orchestration system that runs much of the internet, shows how this evolution happens in practice. Early versions treated all compute resources generically. Modern versions understand GPU resources, can schedule containers based on GPU availability, and even support fractional GPU allocation. Projects like the NVIDIA GPU Operator go further, automatically managing GPU drivers, monitoring, and scheduling across clusters.

But we're still in the early stages. Current systems can schedule based on GPU availability, but they don't understand the nuances of different AI workloads. They can't predict how long a particular model will take to run on specific hardware. They can't dynamically move workloads between NPUs, GPUs, and CPUs based on real-time performance. These capabilities will be essential for AI-native operating systems.

The convergence of AI and system architecture goes beyond individual components. We're seeing the emergence of what might be called "AI-first" system design. Traditional computers were designed with the CPU at the center, surrounded by memory, storage, and peripherals. AI-native systems put neural processing at the center, with traditional computation as a supporting player.

Consider NVIDIA's latest data center designs. They're not just computers with powerful GPUs. They're AI systems that happen to include traditional processors. The high-bandwidth connections between GPUs, the massive parallel memory systems, the specialized interconnects for model parallelism—every architectural decision prioritizes AI workloads. The same principles are scaling down to edge devices, with companies designing chips where the NPU gets first priority for power and memory bandwidth.

This architectural shift reflects a deeper truth: AI computation is not just another workload. It's a fundamentally different kind of computation that demands fundamentally different hardware.

Traditional computing is about control flow—if this, then that. AI computing is about data flow—rivers of numbers flowing through neural networks. Traditional computing prioritizes latency—how fast can we complete one operation? AI computing prioritizes throughput—how many operations can we complete per second?

The hardware industry is responding with remarkable innovation. We're seeing chips with dedicated matrix multiplication units, specialized memory hierarchies for neural network weights, and even analog computing elements that trade precision for efficiency. Some experimental chips can run certain AI models using just milliwatts of power—opening the possibility of AI that runs continuously on battery-powered devices for years.

As these hardware capabilities converge, they enable something unprecedented: operating systems where AI is not an application but the foundation. Where every interaction is processed through neural networks. Where the system learns and adapts continuously. Where privacy is guaranteed by hardware, not just policy. Where intelligent behavior emerges from the architecture itself.

The engineers designing these systems probably feel like the computer pioneers of the 1960s—working at the edge of what's possible, unsure exactly where it will lead but certain it will change everything. They're not just building faster computers. They're building the substrate for a new kind of intelligence, one that merges human intent with computational power in ways we're only beginning to explore.

The next chapter examines how Large Language Models are becoming not just applications that run on this hardware, but computational platforms in their own right. When you combine the architectural principles we've explored with the hardware capabilities now emerging, and then add LLMs as a new kind of computational engine, you get something that transcends traditional notions of what an operating system can be. The pieces are falling into place for a fundamental transformation in how we interact with computers—and how they interact with us.

CHAPTER 6

LLM as a Computing Platform

The moment felt almost anticlimactic. In a San Francisco office in late 2022, an OpenAI engineer typed a simple request into ChatGPT: "Write a Python script to analyze this CSV file and create a visualization of the trends." The AI not only understood the request but generated working code, explained its approach, and offered to refine the results. This wasn't just a chatbot anymore. It was something unprecedented—a new kind of computational engine that understood human intent and could translate it into action.

What made this moment profound wasn't the code generation itself. Plenty of tools could help write code. It was the realization that Large Language Models had become something nobody quite expected: a universal computational platform that could interpret, reason, and create across virtually any domain. We weren't just looking at a better interface. We were looking at a fundamentally new way of computing.

To understand this shift, consider how traditional computers process information. When you run a program, the CPU loads instructions into memory, executes them in sequence, and produces deterministic results. It's a model that hasn't changed fundamentally since von Neumann described it in 1945. But when an LLM processes a prompt, something entirely different happens. There's no traditional program being executed, no sequence of instructions. Instead, billions of neural network parameters work in concert to predict the most likely response, word by word, thought by thought.

The context window of an LLM functions like working memory, but with a crucial difference. Traditional RAM stores exact values—the number 42 is always 42. But the context window holds something richer: meaning, relationships, and intent. When you have a conversation with an LLM, each exchange doesn't just add data to memory; it adds context that colors everything that follows. It's the difference between a filing cabinet that stores documents and a mind that understands them.

This context isn't just passive storage. It actively shapes computation. Ask an LLM to solve a problem, and its approach will be influenced by everything else in the context window—previous examples you've shown, the tone you've established, the domain you're working in. It's as if the memory itself participates in the processing, creating a fluid, adaptive form of computation that would be impossible in traditional architectures.

The limitations of context windows—typically thousands to hundreds of thousands of tokens—might seem like a weakness compared to the gigabytes of RAM in modern computers. But it's actually a feature that mirrors human cognition. We don't hold entire databases in our working memory; we hold the relevant context for the task at hand. The constraint forces focus and relevance, preventing the kind of information overload that plagues traditional systems.

But what happens when we need to store information beyond a single conversation? This is where embeddings revolutionize our concept of storage. In traditional file systems, data exists in rigid formats—documents, images, databases. Embeddings transform any information into high-dimensional vectors that capture meaning rather than just content. It's like the difference between storing a recipe as text versus storing the actual understanding of how flavors combine.

When information is stored as embeddings, retrieval becomes semantic rather than syntactic. Instead of searching for files with specific names or keywords, you can search for concepts, relationships, and meanings. Imagine asking your computer to "find that document about the budget problem we discussed last spring" without remembering its title or where you saved it. The system doesn't just search; it understands what you're looking for.

This semantic storage enables something profound: a file system organized by meaning rather than hierarchy. Related ideas cluster naturally together. Concepts bridge across different documents and media types. The rigid folder structures we've used since the 1960s—descendants of physical filing cabinets—give way to fluid, multidimensional spaces where information exists in context rather than isolation.

The combination of context windows and embeddings creates what we might call "living memory"—storage that understands its contents and can reason about them. It's not just retrieving data; it's reconstructing understanding. Each access doesn't just read information but recontextualizes it based on current needs.

Natural language emerges as the universal interface to this new computational paradigm. For decades, we've forced humans to learn the language of computers—programming languages, command lines, specific syntax. LLMs flip this relationship. The computer learns human language, with all its ambiguity, context, and nuance. It's a democratization more profound than the graphical user interface.

Consider the expressiveness this enables. In traditional interfaces, you're limited to predefined commands and options. Click here, type there, select from this menu. With natural language, you can express not just what you want to do but why, how, and in what context. "Summarize this document focusing on budget implications, but keep the technical details for the engineering team" becomes a valid instruction. The interface understands not just the command but the intent behind it.

This linguistic interface isn't just more flexible—it's more powerful. Traditional interfaces separate thinking from doing. You figure out what you want, then translate it into computer operations. With natural language interfaces, thinking and doing merge. You can refine your request as you go, explore possibilities through conversation, and collaborate with the system rather than just commanding it.

The probabilistic nature of LLMs, initially seen as a limitation, becomes a strength in this new paradigm. Traditional computers give the same answer every time—2 + 2 is always 4. LLMs can give different responses to the same prompt, exploring various approaches and possibilities. This isn't a bug; it's computational creativity. It enables systems that can brainstorm, suggest alternatives, and approach problems from multiple angles.

This probabilistic behavior fundamentally changes how we think about computation. Traditional programming is about control—defining exactly what should happen. LLM-based computation is about guidance—establishing parameters and letting the system find solutions within them. It's like the difference between a train on tracks and a river flowing toward the sea. Both reach their destination, but one adapts to the landscape while the other requires it to be reshaped.

The concept of a probabilistic kernel emerges from this shift. Traditional OS kernels manage deterministic resources—CPU time, memory allocation, file access. A probabilistic kernel would manage uncertainty, context, and meaning. It would schedule not just processes but intentions. It would allocate not just memory but attention. It would control not just access but understanding.

Imagine an operating system kernel that doesn't just respond to system calls but understands objectives. When an application needs resources, it doesn't just request memory; it explains what it's trying to accomplish. The kernel doesn't just grant or deny; it negotiates, suggests alternatives, and optimizes for outcomes rather than just resource usage. It's a kernel that thinks.

This probabilistic kernel would handle failures differently too. Traditional kernels panic when they encounter unexpected states. A probabilistic kernel would gracefully degrade, finding alternative approaches when the primary path fails. It would learn from errors, adapting its behavior over time. Crashes would become rare not because all edge cases are handled but because the system can navigate around them.

The implications cascade through every layer of the system. Device drivers wouldn't just translate between hardware and software; they'd interpret between physical capabilities and user intentions. File systems wouldn't just store data; they'd maintain meaning. Networks wouldn't just move packets; they'd preserve context across distributed computation.

We're witnessing the birth of a new computational paradigm where LLMs aren't just applications running on traditional platforms—they are the platform. The context window is the new RAM. Embeddings are the new file system. Natural language is the new API. Probability is the new determinism.

This isn't just an evolution of existing concepts; it's a fundamental rethinking of what computation means. Traditional computers are tools—powerful but passive, waiting for instructions. LLM-based systems are collaborators—active participants in problem-solving, capable of understanding not just commands but goals, context, and meaning.

The engineers building these systems face challenges that would have seemed nonsensical a decade ago. How do you debug a system that might give different answers each time? How do you ensure reliability when the core computation is probabilistic? How do you maintain security when the boundary between code and data dissolves? These aren't just technical problems—they're philosophical ones that challenge our basic assumptions about computing.

Yet the potential is extraordinary. We're moving toward systems that don't just process information but understand it. That don't just execute commands but grasp intentions. That don't just store data but maintain meaning. It's computing that works the way humans think rather than forcing humans to think the way computers work.

As we stand at this threshold, we can see the outline of operating systems that are truly intelligent—not because they have AI features added, but because intelligence is their fundamental architecture. The next chapters will explore how this theoretical possibility becomes practical reality, transforming every aspect of how we interact with computers. The age of the LLM as a computing platform has arrived, and with it, a new chapter in the story of human-computer collaboration.

Standardizing LLM Context Management - MCP

The transformative potential of large language models (LLMs) as computing platforms hinges on their ability to access and manage context beyond static training data. However, as discussed earlier, fixed context windows and isolated embeddings pose significant limitations, confining LLMs to fragmented interactions. Enter the Model Context Protocol (MCP), an open standard introduced by Anthropic in November 2024, which addresses these constraints by providing a universal framework for bidirectional communication between LLMs and external systems. Often compared to "ODBC for AI"—the Open Database Connectivity standard that revolutionized data access in the 1990s—MCP acts as a secure, standardized connector, enabling LLMs to query, retrieve, and act on real-time data from tools, databases, and services without custom, brittle integrations.

At its core, MCP's mechanics involve three key components: the MCP Client (the LLM or AI agent initiating requests), the MCP Server (an intermediary that translates and secures interactions), and the Service (the actual external resource, such as a semantic file system or hardware monitor). The protocol uses structured, encrypted messages to facilitate context flow: an LLM can send a query (e.g., "Fetch embeddings for budget-related documents"), and the server responds with relevant data streams, complete with metadata for provenance and permissions. This bidirectional nature ensures not just retrieval but also updates—allowing the LLM to push computed results back to storage, creating a dynamic feedback loop. Security is baked in through features like differential privacy, zero-knowledge proofs, and granular access controls, preventing data leaks while supporting federated learning across distributed edges.

This protocol directly enhances the chapter's discussions on context windows and embeddings. Traditional context windows, limited to thousands of tokens, act like short-term memory with rigid boundaries; MCP extends them virtually by enabling on-demand fetching of external embeddings or knowledge graphs. For instance, in a semantic file system, embeddings—those high-dimensional vectors capturing meaning—can be queried semantically via MCP, bridging the gap between stored data and active computation. Instead of reloading entire datasets, the LLM pulls only what's relevant, reducing latency and computational overhead. This mitigates probabilistic uncertainties: by grounding responses in fresh, verifiable external context, outputs become more reliable and less prone to hallucinations, evolving computation from isolated predictions to informed reasoning.

◆ ◆ ◆

The following is an example implementation of Andrej Karpathy LLM OS.

Python LLM OS Example

How the LLM OS Works https://github.com/alessoh/llm-os.git

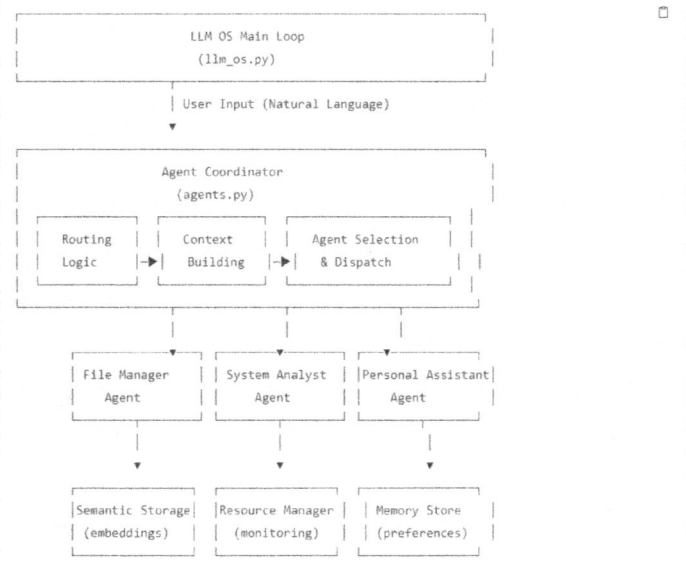

Figure 3 System Architecture Overview

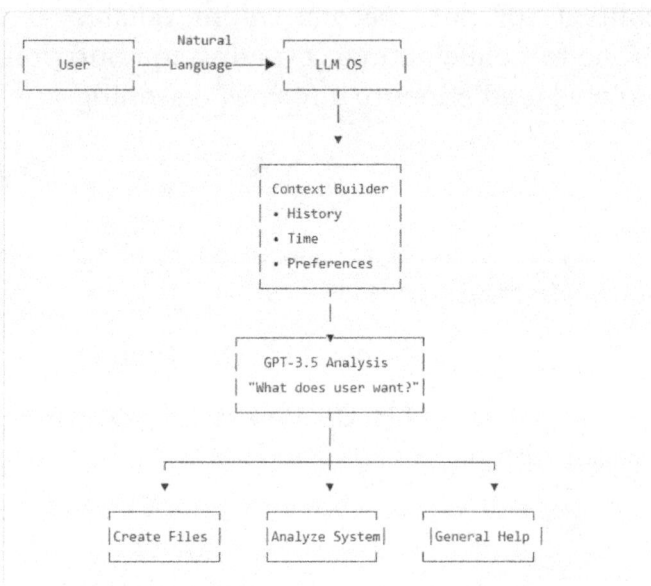

Figure 4 System Operations Overview

README.MD File from project

llm-os
LLM Operating System
LLM OS - AI-Native Operating System

🚀 Features

- **Natural Language Interface**: Communicate with your computer using language
- **Semantic File System**: Files are stored and retrieved based on meaning, not just names
- **Multi-Agent Architecture**: Specialized AI agents handle different types of tasks
- **Context-Aware Assistance**: The system remembers your conversation and preferences
- **Predictive Resource Management**: Monitors and predicts system resource usage
- **Learning System**: Remembers your preferences and improves over time

📑 Table of Contents

- [Quick Start](#-quick-start)
- [System Requirements](#-system-requirements)
- [Detailed Installation](#-detailed-installation)
- [Usage Guide](#-usage-guide)
- [Project Structure](#-project-structure)
- [Troubleshooting](#-troubleshooting)

- [Examples](#-examples)

🚀 Quick Start

For experienced users who want to get running quickly:

```bash
# Clone the repository
git clone https://github.com/alessoh/llm-os.git
cd llm-os

# Create conda environment
conda create -n llmos python=3.9 -y
conda activate llmos

# Quick fix option (no code changes needed)
pip install openai==0.28.1 numpy==1.24.3 scikit-learn==1.3.0 python-dateutil==2.8.2 psutil==5.9.5 colorama==0.4.6

# Set API key and run
set OPENAI_API_KEY=sk-your-key-here
python llm_os.py
```

💻 System Requirements

Hardware
- **RAM**: Minimum 4GB (8GB recommended)
- **Storage**: 1GB free space
- **Processor**: Any modern 64-bit CPU
- **Internet**: Required for API calls

Software

- **OS**: Windows 10/11 (64-bit)
- **Python**: 3.9+ (via Anaconda)
- **OpenAI API Key**: Required (see [Getting an API Key](#getting-openai-api-key))

🔧 Detailed Installation

Step 1: Install Anaconda

1. Download Anaconda from: https://www.anaconda.com/download
2. Run the installer with default settings
3. **Important**: Check "Add Anaconda3 to PATH" during installation
4. Verify installation:
   ```cmd
   conda --version
   ```

Step 2: Get OpenAI API Key

1. Create account at: https://platform.openai.com/
2. Navigate to API keys: https://platform.openai.com/api-keys
3. Click "Create new secret key"
4. Copy the key (starts with `sk-`)
5. Add credits to your account (Settings → Billing)

Step 3: Download LLM OS

Using Git
```cmd
```

```
cd %USERPROFILE%\Documents
git clone https://github.com/alessoh/llm-os.git
cd llm-os
```

Step 4: Set Up Environment

```cmd
# Open Anaconda Prompt and navigate to project
cd %USERPROFILE%\Documents\llm-os

# Create and activate conda environment
conda create -n llmos python=3.9 -y
conda activate llmos
```

Step 5: Install Dependencies

```
pip install -r requirements.txt
```

Step 6: Configure API Key

Method 1: Environment Variable (Quick)
```cmd
set OPENAI_API_KEY=sk-your-actual-key-here
```

Method 2: .env File (Recommended)
```cmd
# Create .env file from template
copy .env.example .env
```

```
# Edit .env file and add your key
notepad .env
```

Step 7: Verify Setup

```cmd
# Run the verification script
python test_setup.py
```

You should see all green checkmarks (✓). If not, see [Troubleshooting](#-troubleshooting).

Step 8: Run LLM OS

```cmd
python llm_os.py
```

🚀 Usage Guide

Basic Commands

Once running, you can interact naturally:

```
You> Create a document about machine learning basics
You> Find all my Python notes
You> What's using the most CPU right now?
You> Remember that I prefer markdown format
You> Help me organize my project files
```

```

### Special Commands
- `help` - Show available commands and examples
- `exit` or `quit` - Exit the program

### Example Session
```

==

LLM OS - AI-Native Operating System Demo

==

[System] Initializing LLM OS...
[System] API connection successful!
[System] LLM OS initialized successfully!
[System] Type 'help' for available commands or just chat naturally.

You> Create a note about my project ideas

[FileManager] Created document file_20240120_143022 with content:

Project Ideas

Here are some innovative project concepts to explore:

1. **Smart Home Automation**
   - Voice-controlled lighting system
   - Automated temperature management...

You> What's my CPU usage?

[SystemAnalyst] Current system analysis:

CPU Usage: 15.2% (Predicted in 30s: 17.8%)
Memory Usage: 42.3% (6.8 GB available)

Top Process: chrome.exe using 8.5% CPU

Your system is running smoothly with plenty of resources available.

You> Remember I prefer markdown format for docs

[Assistant] I'll remember that your preference is markdown format for docs

You> exit

[System] Shutting down LLM OS...
[System] Conversation history saved.
[System] Goodbye!
```

## ☐ Project Structure
```
llm-os/
├── llm_os.py   # Main program entry point
├── agents.py   # AI agent implementations
├── semantic_storage.py   # Semantic file system
├── resource_manager.py   # System resource monitoring

```
├── config.py          # Configuration settings
├── utils.py           # Utility functions
├── requirements.txt   # Python dependencies
├── test_setup.py      # Setup verification script
├── auto_fix.py        # Automatic code fixer
├── .env.example       # Environment variable template
├── .gitignore         # Git ignore rules
└── README.md          # This file
```

Generated Files

When you run LLM OS, it creates:
```
llm_os_storage/
├── metadata.json              # File metadata
├── embeddings.json            # Semantic embeddings
└── conversation_history.json  # Chat history
```

🔧 Troubleshooting

Common Issues

"conda is not recognized"
- Use **Anaconda Prompt** not Command Prompt
- Restart computer after Anaconda installation
- Reinstall Anaconda with PATH option checked

"No module named 'openai'"

```cmd
conda activate llmos
pip install -r requirements.txt
```

"OpenAI API key not found!"
```cmd
# Check if key is set
echo %OPENAI_API_KEY%

# If blank, set it:
set OPENAI_API_KEY=sk-your-actual-key
```

API Error 401 (Unauthorized)
- Verify API key starts with `sk-`
- Check key validity at: https://platform.openai.com/api-keys
- Ensure you have credits in your account

API Error 429 (Rate Limit)
- Wait 60 seconds before retrying
- Check usage at: https://platform.openai.com/usage

"Python was not found"
```cmd
# Ensure conda environment is active
conda activate llmos
```

Advanced Troubleshooting

Run the diagnostic script:

```cmd
python test_setup.py
```

This will check:
- ✓ Python version
- ✓ Required packages
- ✓ API key configuration
- ✓ OpenAI connection
- ✓ Project files

⬜ Examples

File Operations
- `"Create a Python script for data analysis"`
- `"Find all documents about neural networks"`
- `"Show me files I created yesterday"`
- `"Help me organize my research papers"`

System Analysis
- `"What's my current memory usage?"`
- `"Which programs are using the most resources?"`
- `"Analyze my system performance"`
- `"Predict CPU usage for the next minute"`

Personal Assistant
- `"Remember that I'm working on a web project"`
- `"What preferences have you learned about me?"`
- `"Summarize our conversation"`
- `"Help me plan my coding tasks"`

Configuration

Environment Variables

Create a `.env` file in the project root:
```env
# Required
OPENAI_API_KEY=sk-your-api-key-here

# Optional
OPENAI_MODEL=gpt-3.5-turbo
OPENAI_EMBEDDING_MODEL=text-embedding-ada-002
```

Available Models

Edit `config.py` to change models:
```python
# Default (fast and cheap)
MODEL_NAME = "gpt-3.5-turbo"

# Latest GPT-3.5
MODEL_NAME = "gpt-3.5-turbo-0125"

# More capable
MODEL_NAME = "gpt-4o-mini"

# Most capable
MODEL_NAME = "gpt-4-turbo-preview"
```

Cost Estimation

- Each interaction: ~$0.002 (GPT-3.5-turbo)

- 100 interactions: ~$0.20
  - 1000 interactions: ~$2.00

Monitor usage at: https://platform.openai.com/usage

Contributing

This is a demonstration project. Feel free to:
- Fork and experiment
- Submit issues for bugs
- Share your modifications
- Build upon the concepts

License

This project is provided as-is for educational purposes. See the repository for license details.

Additional Resources

- **Repository**: https://github.com/alessoh/llm-os
- **OpenAI Docs**: https://platform.openai.com/docs
- **Anaconda Help**: https://docs.anaconda.com/
- **Python Tutorial**: https://docs.python.org/3/tutorial/

⚠ Important Notes

- **Internet Required**: The system needs internet for API calls
- **Privacy**: Commands are processed by

OpenAI's servers
   - **Costs**: OpenAI API usage incurs charges
   - **Educational**: This is a demonstration, not production software

   ---

CHAPTER 7

Conversational Interfaces

Consider the following hypothetical:

Sarah stares at her monitor, fingers hovering over the keyboard. She needs to find a presentation she'd created months ago—something about quarterly metrics, with a blue theme, probably made sometime after the Tokyo conference but before the budget review. In a traditional file system, this would mean clicking through dozens of folders, opening files to check their contents, trying to remember what she might have named it. Instead, she simply types: "Find that presentation I made about metrics after the Tokyo trip—the one with the blue charts."

Her computer understands. Not through keyword matching or clever search algorithms, but through genuine comprehension of her request. It knew when the Tokyo conference was, understood that "blue charts" referred to the visual theme, and could infer the likely timeframe. Within seconds, it presents not just the file but context: "Here's your Q3 metrics presentation from April 15th. You presented this to the board on April 20th. Would you like me to update the data with current figures?"

This interaction would represent a fundamental shift in how humans and computers communicate. We're moving beyond the rigid paradigms that have defined computing for decades —command lines that demand perfect syntax and graphical interfaces that force us into predetermined paths. We're entering an era of genuine conversation with our machines.

The command line, beloved by engineers and system administrators, represents pure functionality stripped of pretense. Every interaction follows a strict grammar: command, flags, arguments. Type 'ls -la /home/user' and you'll see a directory listing. Mistype it as 'sl -la /home/user' and you'll get an error. There's no forgiveness, no interpretation, no understanding— just mechanical parsing of text strings.

This rigidity has its virtues. Command lines are powerful, predictable, and scriptable. They allow precise control over system behavior. But they also create a priesthood of computing—those who have memorized the incantations and those who haven't. The learning curve isn't just steep; it's a cliff face that many users never attempt to climb.

Graphical user interfaces promised to democratize computing, and in many ways they succeeded. Point, click, drag, drop—these interactions map naturally to how we manipulate objects in physical space. But GUIs brought their own limitations. Every action must be anticipated by designers and exposed through menus, buttons, or gestures. You can only do what the interface allows, following paths predetermined by someone who couldn't possibly anticipate every user's needs.

Consider the absurdity of modern GUI interactions. To rename multiple files, you might need to select each one individually, right-click, choose rename, type the new name, hit enter, then repeat. Or you could open a terminal and type a single command—if you know the magic words. The GUI makes simple things easy and complex things impossible. The command line makes everything possible but nothing easy.

Conversational interfaces transcend this dichotomy. They combine the accessibility of GUIs with the power of command lines, then add something neither possessed: understanding. When you tell an AI-native operating system to "organize my photos from last summer's vacation," you don't need to specify file formats, directory structures, or sorting algorithms. The system understands what a vacation is, can identify timeframes, and knows how humans typically like to organize memories.

This understanding operates at the OS level, not

as an application layer. Traditional systems process commands mechanically—parse the text, match it to functions, execute predefined operations. AI-native systems process meaning. They understand that "clean up my desktop" might mean organizing files by type, archiving old documents, and removing duplicates. They grasp that "prepare for my morning meeting" could involve opening relevant documents, checking for updates from team members, and adjusting system resources for video conferencing.

The natural language understanding goes beyond simple command interpretation. It includes pragmatics—the contextual aspects of communication that humans take for granted. When you say "make this bigger," the system understands from context whether you mean font size, window dimensions, or image resolution. When you ask to "send this to John," it knows which John based on your recent interactions and current project context.

But humans don't communicate through text alone. We gesture, point, speak with tone and emotion, and share visual information. AI-native operating systems embrace this multi-modal reality. You might start a request by speaking aloud, clarify with a gesture captured by camera, and refine by typing specific details. The system doesn't treat these as separate inputs but as facets of a single communicative act.

Imagine editing a video by describing your intent rather than clicking through timelines and effects panels. "Start with the sunrise shot, fade to the interview, but make it feel more optimistic." You gesture to indicate pacing, speak to set mood, and type to specify exact timestamps when needed. The system integrates all these inputs, understanding not just what you want but why you want it.

Voice interaction in this context transcends the simple command-and-response patterns of current assistants. It becomes truly conversational, with the system maintaining context across extended exchanges. You don't need to repeat information or re-establish context with each utterance. The conversation flows naturally, with the system asking clarifying questions when needed and offering suggestions based on understanding your goals.

Visual input adds another dimension. Point a camera at a broken device, and the system doesn't just identify it—it understands you likely need repair instructions, replacement part orders, or troubleshooting help. Show it a sketch of a interface design, and it can generate working code that captures your intent, not just the literal lines on paper. The visual becomes another channel of communication, processed alongside language and gesture.

This multi-modal processing happens continuously and ambiently. The system doesn't wait for explicit commands but maintains awareness of context. It notices when you're struggling with a task and offers help. It sees you're preparing for travel and suggests relevant preparations. It hears frustration in your voice and adjusts its interaction style

AI OPERATING SYSTEMS

accordingly. The interface becomes less about issuing commands and more about ongoing collaboration.

Context preservation transforms these interactions from isolated exchanges to coherent conversations. Traditional interfaces have no memory—each command starts fresh. Even modern assistants typically reset context between sessions. But AI-native systems maintain rich, persistent context that spans not just minutes but months.

This context isn't just a transcript of past interactions. It's a structured understanding of your projects, goals, relationships, and patterns. When you return to a task after weeks away, the system remembers not just what you were doing but why you were doing it, what challenges you faced, and what you planned to do next. It's like having a collaborator with perfect memory but infinite patience.

The context spans across applications and workflows. Start writing an email about a project, and the system understands connections to related documents, previous conversations, and upcoming deadlines. It doesn't just autocomplete words—it anticipates needs, suggests relevant information, and helps maintain consistency across all your work on that project.

This persistence enables something remarkable: the system learns your communication style. Not just your vocabulary or common phrases, but your patterns of thought, your preferred ways of organizing information, your typical workflows. It adapts its responses to match your style while gently expanding your capabilities. It's personalization not through settings and preferences but through understanding and adaptation.

Privacy becomes paramount in this world of persistent context and continuous understanding. The system must maintain boundaries between different aspects of your life, understanding when you're wearing your professional hat versus personal one. It must forget when asked, maintain confidences, and never leak context across security boundaries. The conversational interface must be not just intelligent but trustworthy.

The challenges of building such interfaces are immense. How do you handle ambiguity when the stakes are high? What happens when the system misunderstands in ways that could cause damage? How do you provide the predictability users need while maintaining the flexibility conversation allows? These aren't just technical problems but design challenges that require rethinking fundamental assumptions about human-computer interaction.

Yet the potential is transformative. We're moving from interfaces that constrain us to interfaces that empower us. From systems that require us to think like computers to systems that think like humans. From tools that process our commands to collaborators that understand our goals.

The university student who struggles with command line syntax can accomplish complex tasks through natural conversation. The executive who doesn't have time to learn new software can simply explain what they need. The artist who thinks visually can communicate through sketches and gestures. The engineer who needs precision can still access it, but within a context of understanding rather than rigid syntax.

As these conversational interfaces mature, they're changing not just how we interact with computers but how we think about them. They're no longer tools we use but entities we communicate with. Not servants following orders but collaborators in problem-solving. The boundary between user and system blurs as interaction becomes conversation and commands become dialogue.

The next chapter explores how this conversational capability combines with proactive intelligence to create systems that don't just respond to our needs but anticipate them. When natural language understanding meets predictive resource management, we get operating systems that are not just reactive but truly helpful—preparing for our needs before we express them, optimizing for our goals before we articulate them. The conversation is just beginning.

CHAPTER 8

Proactive Resource Management

We've all experienced it—that moment when your computer decides to update, scan for viruses, or index files right when you're in the middle of critical work. Your machine, equipped with processors powerful enough to simulate molecular interactions, grinds to a halt because the operating system scheduled maintenance at the worst possible time. It's a maddening reminder that our computers, for all their computational might, have no understanding of what we're trying to accomplish.

This frustration stems from a fundamental architectural limitation: operating systems are reactive. They wait for applications to request resources, then scramble to provide them. They respond to events as they occur, with no memory of what happened yesterday and no anticipation of what might happen next. It's like running a hospital that only orders supplies after patients arrive, rather than maintaining inventory based on predictable patterns.

The tragedy is that our computing patterns are remarkably predictable. Data scientists run similar workloads at regular times. Video editors follow consistent workflows. Office workers have meeting schedules that repeat weekly. Our computers have access to all this information—calendar appointments, file access patterns, application usage histories—yet they treat each moment as if encountering it for the first time.

Traditional operating systems manage resources through algorithms designed in an era of scarce memory and single-core processors. The scheduler gives each process a fair share of CPU time. The memory manager allocates RAM as requested. The I/O system processes disk operations in the order received. These approaches made sense when computers ran a handful of simple programs. They're wholly inadequate for modern workloads where a single application might spawn hundreds of threads across dozens of CPU cores while streaming gigabytes of data.

AI-native operating systems transform this reactive model into something proactive and intelligent. Instead of waiting for resource requests, they predict them. Instead of treating each application as an isolated entity, they understand workflows and patterns. Instead of optimizing for fairness, they optimize for outcomes.

The foundation of this transformation is pattern recognition applied to system behavior. Every time you open an application, access a file, or start a task, you're creating data. Traditional systems discard this information after basic logging. AI-native systems learn from it. They build models of your behavior—not to invade privacy, but to serve you better.

These models capture subtleties that rigid algorithms miss. They learn that certain email subjects correlate with urgent computational needs. They recognize that opening specific project files signals the start of resource-intensive work. They understand that your usage patterns shift when deadlines approach or when collaborating with certain teams. It's machine learning applied not to abstract datasets but to the practical challenge of making computers more helpful.

Predictive scheduling emerges from this understanding. Instead of merely deciding which process runs next, the scheduler anticipates what processes will need to run. It sees you open a development environment and predicts compilation will follow. It notices you're joining a video call and ensures audio and video processing have priority. It learns that you run data analysis scripts every morning and pre-allocates resources before you even log in.

This prediction extends to entire computational pipelines. Modern workflows rarely involve single applications—they're chains of tools working together. Video production moves from editing to rendering to encoding to uploading. Software development cycles through coding, compiling, testing, and deploying. AI-native systems understand these pipelines and prepare resources for each stage before it's needed.

Memory management becomes similarly intelligent. Traditional systems allocate memory when requested and free it when released, leading to fragmentation and inefficiency. Predictive memory management anticipates needs based on patterns. It pre-loads frequently used libraries. It maintains hot caches of commonly accessed data. It even predicts memory usage spikes and ensures sufficient free RAM is available before the demand arrives.

Power management on mobile devices showcases the practical benefits of this approach. Current systems use crude heuristics—reduce performance on battery, boost when plugged in. Predictive power management learns your actual usage patterns. It understands the difference between active work sessions and idle periods. It can provide full performance during critical tasks while aggressively conserving power when you're just reading. Battery life improves not through bigger batteries but through smarter resource allocation.

The learning process respects privacy while capturing patterns. Federated learning allows systems to improve their predictions based on aggregate behavior without exposing individual data.

Differential privacy ensures that models capture general patterns without memorizing specific details. Local processing keeps sensitive information on your device while still enabling intelligent prediction. It's possible to have systems that learn without surveilling.

Network resources benefit particularly from prediction. Traditional systems request data when needed, leading to delays. Predictive systems can pre-fetch information based on patterns. They know which files you typically access after opening certain documents. They understand which cloud resources correlate with specific projects. They can even predict network congestion and route traffic accordingly. The result is networks that feel faster without actually increasing bandwidth.

Storage systems transform from passive repositories to active participants in workflow optimization. They learn which files cluster together in actual use, regardless of folder structure. They understand temporal patterns—which documents you need at month-end, which resources are accessed seasonally. They can move data between storage tiers predictively, ensuring fast access to what you'll need next while archiving what you won't.

The impact on system performance is dramatic but often invisible. Applications seem to launch instantly—not because of faster hardware but because the system predicted you'd need them. Files open without delay because the system cached them in advance. Complex workflows complete faster because resources were pre-positioned at each stage. It's optimization that users experience as "everything just works."

This extends beyond individual machines to distributed systems. In office environments, patterns emerge across users and time. Monday mornings see heavy email and document usage. Friday afternoons shift toward creative work. Month-end brings reporting and analysis. AI-native systems can recognize these patterns and optimize accordingly—scheduling updates during genuinely quiet periods, pre-caching commonly needed resources, balancing loads across infrastructure.

Security systems gain new capabilities through pattern learning. Traditional antivirus scans files against known threats. Predictive security learns normal behavior so well that anomalies immediately stand out. It's not just checking against a blacklist but understanding what legitimate behavior looks like for each user and application. This enables detection of novel threats that signature-based systems miss.

The challenges of predictive resource management are substantial. Incorrect predictions waste resources and potentially degrade performance. Novel situations require graceful fallbacks to reactive mode. Users need transparency about what's being learned and control over how predictions influence system behavior. The system must balance between being helpful and being intrusive.

Yet the benefits are transformative. We're

witnessing the emergence of operating systems that feel genuinely intelligent. They remove the friction of resource management, letting users focus on goals rather than system administration. They optimize not for abstract metrics but for human productivity and satisfaction.

The distance between reactive and proactive resource management is the distance between tool and assistant. Traditional operating systems are powerful tools that respond to commands. AI-native systems are intelligent assistants that anticipate needs. They don't just manage resources—they enable outcomes.

As we perfect these predictive capabilities, we're approaching something profound: systems that help users discover better workflows. By understanding patterns deeply, they can suggest optimizations users haven't considered. They might recommend better times for certain tasks based on productivity patterns. They might identify automation opportunities in repetitive workflows. They become not just responsive to how we work but helpful in improving how we work.

The next chapter explores how this intelligence transforms storage from rigid hierarchies to fluid, semantic spaces. When predictive intelligence meets semantic understanding, we get file systems that organize by meaning rather than manual categorization. The future of computing isn't just about managing resources more intelligently—it's about understanding information itself.

CHAPTER 9

Intelligent File Systems

The file system is perhaps computing's most successful metaphor. Files and folders, borrowed from office furniture, gave early computer users an intuitive way to organize digital information. But this metaphor, designed when computers stored dozens of documents, now strains under the weight of millions of files. We've reached the limits of what hierarchical organization can offer, and artificial intelligence points toward something radically different.

Consider how we currently organize information. We create elaborate folder structures, trying to anticipate every way we might want to find something later. Documents/Projects/2024/ClientName/ProjectType/Version3/Final/ReallyFinal/. We give files names that try to capture their essence in a few words, hoping we'll remember our naming convention months later. When that fails, we resort to desktop search, typing fragments of text we hope exist somewhere in the document.

This approach worked when information was scarce. It fails catastrophically in an era of abundance. The average knowledge worker manages thousands of files across multiple devices and cloud services. The careful taxonomies we create become prisons, forcing us to remember not just what we stored but how we chose to categorize it. Finding information becomes an exercise in archaeology, digging through layers of organizational sediment.

The fundamental problem is that traditional file systems organize by structure rather than meaning. They care about where files are stored, not what they contain. They treat a groundbreaking research paper and a grocery list with equal incomprehension—both are just sequences of bytes with names attached. This structural blindness makes semantic operations impossible. You can't ask for "all documents related to the Johnson project" unless you've explicitly tagged them or stored them together.

Embeddings offer a radical alternative. In machine learning, embeddings are high-dimensional numerical representations that capture the semantic meaning of content. When text, images, or other data are converted to embeddings, similar content naturally clusters together in this mathematical space. A research paper about quantum computing and a presentation on the same topic would have similar embeddings, even if they share no common keywords or file properties.

This isn't theoretical—embedding technology exists today in search engines, recommendation systems, and language models. What's new is imagining embeddings as the primary organization principle for file systems. Instead of storing files in folders, we'd store them in semantic space. Instead of hierarchical paths, we'd have multidimensional relationships. Instead of rigid categories, we'd have fluid associations.

In such a system, every piece of content would be understood at the moment of storage. Text documents would be processed by language models to extract meaning, themes, and relationships. Images would be analyzed for content, style, and context. Code would be understood in terms of functionality and dependencies. Even binary files would be characterized by their purpose and associations. The file system wouldn't just store data—it would comprehend it.

Semantic search becomes natural in this environment. Rather than searching for file names or specific text strings, users could search by meaning. "Find all documents discussing our pricing strategy" would return relevant results regardless of whether they contain the word "pricing" or are stored in a "strategy" folder. "Show me images similar to this sketch" would find conceptually related pictures, not just visually identical ones.

The power extends beyond simple retrieval. Semantic file systems could answer complex queries that are impossible today. "What documents contradict our current marketing message?" requires understanding not just content but relationships and implications. "Find all code that might be affected by this API change" needs comprehension of programming semantics. These queries move from information retrieval to knowledge synthesis.

Traditional file names become almost irrelevant in this model. Why struggle to encode meaning in a few dozen characters when the system understands the full content? Files could be referenced by their semantic fingerprint rather than arbitrary names. Users might still assign human-readable labels for convenience, but these would be more like nicknames than unique identifiers. The system would understand that "quarterly report," "Q3 analysis," and "sales figures for last quarter" might all refer to the same document.

This semantic understanding enables organization that adapts to context. The same document might appear in different virtual "locations" depending on how you're accessing it. When working on a budget, financial documents naturally surface. When preparing a presentation, relevant slides and images cluster together. The organization isn't fixed but fluid, reshaping based on current needs and relationships.

Version control in semantic file systems moves beyond tracking textual differences to understanding conceptual evolution. Current version control systems can tell you that line 47 changed from "x =

5" to "x = 6". Semantic version control could explain that "the discount rate was increased to reflect market conditions." It could track not just what changed but why, maintaining a conceptual history of document evolution.

This conceptual versioning extends to all content types. For images, it might track that "the color scheme was adjusted to match brand guidelines." For code, it could note that "the authentication logic was refactored for better security." For presentations, it might record that "slides 5-8 were reorganized to improve narrative flow." Version history becomes a story of ideas rather than a log of character changes.

The implications for collaboration are profound. When multiple people work on related content, the system could automatically identify overlaps, conflicts, and synergies. It might notice that two team members are writing similar sections and suggest they coordinate. It could flag when a new document contradicts established information elsewhere. It could even identify knowledge gaps—areas where documentation should exist but doesn't.

Privacy and access control gain new dimensions in semantic systems. Instead of simple read/write permissions, you could grant semantic access. "Allow access to technical specifications but not financial projections" becomes possible when the system understands content meaning. Sensitive information could be automatically identified and protected based on its semantic signature rather than manual classification.

The challenges of building semantic file systems are significant. Processing every file to extract meaning requires substantial computational resources. Embeddings for large documents or high-resolution media can be expensive to generate and store. Semantic understanding must be accurate enough to be reliable while handling the full diversity of human-generated content. Different users might have different semantic interpretations of the same content.

Yet the benefits justify the effort. We're approaching a world where information finds you rather than you hunting for it. Where organization emerges from meaning rather than being imposed through hierarchy. Where the computer understands your information space as well as you do—perhaps better, given its perfect memory and ability to perceive patterns across vast scales.

Research in this area is advancing rapidly. Vector databases optimized for embedding storage and retrieval are becoming mainstream. Language models capable of understanding diverse content types are improving monthly. Efficient algorithms for semantic search across billions of items are being deployed at scale. The pieces needed for semantic file systems are falling into place.

The transition from hierarchical to semantic organization represents more than a technical upgrade. It's a fundamental shift in how we relate to information. Current file systems force us to be librarians, carefully cataloging and organizing. Semantic systems let us be explorers, discovering connections and insights. The cognitive burden of information management lifts, replaced by the creative opportunity of information synthesis.

As semantic file systems mature, they'll enable new forms of knowledge work. Researchers could explore conceptual spaces rather than keyword searches. Writers could find inspiration through semantic associations rather than manual browsing. Programmers could understand system dependencies through meaning rather than documentation. The file system becomes not just storage but an active partner in intellectual work.

The next chapter explores how this semantic understanding combines with security innovations to create systems that are both more open and more protective. When the system understands what information means, it can make intelligent decisions about who should access it and how. Security moves from rigid rules to semantic comprehension, enabling collaboration while protecting privacy. The future of file systems isn't just smarter—it's fundamentally more helpful.

CHAPTER 10

Security in the AI Era

Security has always been an arms race. Attackers develop new techniques, defenders create countermeasures, and the cycle continues. But we've reached an inflection point where traditional security approaches—signature-based detection, rule-based firewalls, static permissions—can no longer keep pace with the sophistication and scale of modern threats. AI-native operating systems don't just add intelligence to security; they fundamentally reimagine what security means and how it works.

Traditional antivirus software operates like a wanted poster system. It maintains vast databases of known malware signatures—specific patterns of code that identify malicious software. When it scans a file, it's essentially comparing mugshots. This worked when malware was relatively static and distribution was slow. Today, attackers use polymorphic code that changes its signature with each infection, automated tools that generate millions of variants, and zero-day exploits that have never been seen before. The wanted poster approach fails when criminals constantly change their faces.

AI-driven threat detection abandons the futile chase of cataloging every possible threat. Instead, it learns what normal looks like and identifies deviations. This isn't simple anomaly detection—it's deep behavioral understanding. The system learns the typical patterns of every process, application, and user interaction. It understands not just what programs do, but how they do it, building rich models of legitimate behavior.

When a word processor suddenly starts encrypting files en masse, traditional antivirus might not flag it—encryption isn't inherently malicious. But AI-driven security understands that this behavior is anomalous for a word processor. It recognizes the pattern of ransomware even if it's never seen this specific variant. It can intervene before damage occurs, not because it recognizes a signature, but because it understands intent.

This intelligence operates at every level of the system. Network traffic analysis moves beyond port numbers and protocols to understand communication patterns. A command-and-control channel might use standard HTTPS, indistinguishable from legitimate traffic by traditional means. But AI security notices subtle patterns—timing irregularities, payload characteristics, behavioral anomalies—that reveal malicious intent. It's like having a security expert who can spot a lie not from the words spoken but from the way they're delivered.

The kernel level—the deepest, most privileged part of the operating system—presents unique challenges and opportunities for AI security. Traditional kernels are deterministic, making security decisions based on fixed rules. AI-native kernels can implement behavioral analysis at the most fundamental level, watching how processes interact with system resources and identifying suspicious patterns before they escalate.

This kernel-level intelligence enables unprecedented visibility. Every system call, every memory access, every hardware interaction flows through the kernel. AI models can analyze these patterns in real-time, building behavioral profiles for every process. A legitimate browser accessing network resources looks different from malware pretending to be a browser. The subtle differences in timing, resource usage, and system call patterns create fingerprints that AI can distinguish even when traditional methods cannot.

The behavioral analysis extends to user interactions. Traditional security treats users as static entities with fixed permissions. AI security understands that users have patterns—when they work, what they access, how they interact with systems. When someone logs in from an unusual location at an odd time and immediately accesses sensitive files they've never touched before, the system doesn't just log an event—it understands the anomaly and can respond appropriately.

But this deep behavioral understanding raises a paradox: the more a system knows about behavior, the more it potentially invades privacy. This is where privacy-preserving computation becomes essential. Technologies like homomorphic encryption, secure multi-party computation, and trusted execution environments allow AI systems to analyze patterns without accessing raw data. It's like a doctor diagnosing illness from symptoms without conducting invasive procedures.

Confidential computing hardware, discussed in earlier chapters, provides the foundation for this privacy-preserving analysis. Intel's TDX and AMD's SEV-SNP create secure enclaves where sensitive data can be processed without exposure to the rest of the system. AI models can train on encrypted data, producing insights without ever "seeing" the raw information. This isn't theoretical—major cloud providers now offer confidential computing services, and the technology is rapidly maturing.

The true power emerges when these privacy-preserving techniques enable collaborative security through federated learning. Traditional security operates in silos—each organization fights threats alone, learning from its own experiences. Federated learning allows organizations to collectively train security models without sharing sensitive data. Each participant contributes model updates derived from their local threat intelligence, creating shared defense without shared vulnerability.

Imagine hospitals collaborating to detect healthcare-specific cyberattacks. Each institution sees different attack patterns, but patient privacy prevents sharing raw security logs. With federated learning, each hospital trains local models on their threat data. They share only the model improvements—mathematical updates that reveal patterns but not specifics. The collective intelligence improves everyone's security without compromising anyone's privacy.

This collaborative approach extends beyond organizations to create ecosystem-wide immunity. When one system detects a novel attack pattern, it can contribute that knowledge to the collective defense without revealing what was attacked or how. It's like a distributed immune system where antibodies developed in one organism benefit the entire population. The speed of defense propagation matches the speed of attack distribution.

The financial sector demonstrates the potential. Banks face sophisticated, coordinated attacks that evolve rapidly. Traditional information sharing is slow and limited by competitive concerns. Federated learning allows real-time collaboration—when one bank's AI detects a new fraud pattern, all participating banks can defend against it within hours, not weeks. The attackers lose their advantage of hitting multiple targets with the same technique.

But federated learning for security faces unique challenges. Adversarial participants might try to poison the collective model with bad updates. The system must verify contributions without seeing their content. Different organizations have different security postures and risk tolerances. Balancing collective benefit with individual needs requires sophisticated protocols and governance structures.

Privacy-preserving computation also enables new forms of security services. Security vendors can offer AI-powered threat detection that operates entirely on customer infrastructure without accessing customer data. Regulatory compliance can be verified through zero-knowledge proofs—mathematically demonstrating compliance without revealing underlying data. Incident response can be automated while maintaining chain-of-custody requirements for digital evidence.

The convergence of AI and security transforms incident response from reactive to predictive. Traditional incident response begins after a breach is detected. AI-driven systems can identify attack precursors—the subtle reconnaissance and probing that precede actual attacks. They can predict likely attack vectors based on observed patterns and proactively strengthen defenses. It's the difference between waiting for symptoms and preventing disease.

This predictive capability extends to zero-day vulnerabilities—previously unknown software flaws that attackers exploit. Traditional security can't defend against unknown vulnerabilities by definition. But AI systems can identify the behavioral patterns of zero-day exploitation even without knowing the specific vulnerability. They recognize that software is being manipulated in unexpected ways and can intervene based on behavioral anomalies rather than signature matching.

The challenges of AI-era security are as significant as the opportunities. AI models themselves become attack targets—adversarial examples can fool image recognition, and model extraction attacks can steal intellectual property. The systems must defend not just against traditional attacks but against AI-specific threats. Security models must be robust against poisoning, evasion, and manipulation.

Explainability becomes crucial for security AI. When a system blocks an action or flags a threat, administrators need to understand why. Black-box AI decisions are unacceptable in security contexts where false positives can disrupt business and false negatives can be catastrophic. The challenge is maintaining explainability while preserving the sophisticated pattern recognition that makes AI security effective.

Yet the trajectory is clear. We're moving from security as a set of rules to security as continuous understanding. From protecting perimeters to protecting behaviors. From isolated defenses to collective intelligence. From reactive patching to proactive immunity. AI doesn't just improve security—it transforms what security means.

The next chapter explores how this

transformation extends beyond security to reshape the fundamental nature of work. When operating systems can understand intent, anticipate needs, and collaborate intelligently, they don't just protect our data—they amplify our capabilities. The AI era isn't just about defending against threats; it's about enabling possibilities we're only beginning to imagine.

CHAPTER 11

Enterprise AI Platforms

The transformation of operating systems from traditional architectures to AI-native designs doesn't happen in isolation. Across the enterprise landscape, platforms are emerging that bridge the gap between current infrastructure and the AI-powered future. These aren't merely tools or frameworks—they're complete ecosystems that demonstrate how AI workloads fundamentally differ from traditional computing and require new approaches to orchestration, deployment, and management.

NVIDIA's approach to enterprise AI platforms reveals the depth of change required. Their DRIVE AGX platform for autonomous vehicles isn't just powerful hardware—it's a complete rethinking of how computational platforms work when AI is the primary workload. Traditional automotive computing focused on deterministic control systems with strict timing requirements. DRIVE AGX must handle multiple neural networks processing sensor data in real-time while maintaining the safety guarantees required for vehicles.

The architecture reflects AI-first thinking. Multiple specialized processors handle different aspects of perception, planning, and control. The system can process data from dozens of cameras, lidar sensors, and radar units simultaneously. But what makes it truly revolutionary is the software stack that orchestrates these resources. It doesn't just schedule processes—it understands the AI pipeline from sensor input to vehicle control, optimizing data flow and computation for minimal latency.

NVIDIA's Isaac platform for robotics takes similar principles into industrial and service environments. Robots present unique challenges for AI platforms—they must process sensory data, plan movements, and execute actions in dynamic environments where mistakes can cause physical damage. Isaac provides not just computational power but an entire ecosystem for developing, training, and deploying robotic AI systems.

The simulation capabilities of Isaac demonstrate why traditional platforms fall short for AI workloads. Before deploying AI models to physical robots, they must be trained and tested extensively. Isaac includes photorealistic simulation environments where robots can learn through millions of iterations without wear, tear, or safety risks. The platform seamlessly bridges simulation and reality, allowing models trained in virtual environments to transfer to physical robots.

These specialized platforms highlight a crucial reality: AI workloads aren't just another type of application. They require fundamentally different approaches to resource management, data handling, and system architecture. This reality has driven the evolution of more general-purpose platforms like Kubernetes to accommodate AI requirements.

Kubernetes began as a container orchestration system, automating the deployment and management of containerized applications across clusters of machines. Its original design focused on web services and traditional applications—stateless processes that could be easily replicated and load-balanced. AI workloads shattered these assumptions. Training a large neural network isn't stateless—it involves gigabytes of model parameters updated through iterative processes. It can't be arbitrarily interrupted and restarted. It requires specific hardware like GPUs that aren't interchangeable with regular processors.

The Kubernetes community responded with extensions and modifications that acknowledge AI's unique requirements. GPU scheduling became a first-class concern, with the ability to request specific GPU types and quantities. Persistent volume management evolved to handle the large datasets common in machine learning. Job scheduling gained sophistication to handle long-running training tasks that might take days or weeks to complete.

Kubeflow emerged as a dedicated platform for machine learning workflows on Kubernetes. It recognizes that AI development isn't just about running models—it's an entire pipeline from data preparation through training to deployment. Kubeflow provides tools for each stage, integrated into cohesive workflows that can be versioned, shared, and reproduced.

The pipeline abstraction in Kubeflow represents a conceptual shift in how we think about AI computation. Traditional software development produces static artifacts—compiled binaries or interpreted scripts. AI development produces models that are intimately tied to their training data, hyperparameters, and computational environment. Kubeflow pipelines capture this entire context, making AI development reproducible and auditable.

Container orchestration for AI workloads presents challenges that reveal the limitations of current operating systems. Containers were designed for process isolation and resource limitation—keeping applications from interfering with each other. But AI workloads often need to share resources in sophisticated ways. Multiple processes might need coordinated access to GPU memory. Distributed training requires high-bandwidth communication between containers. The isolation that makes containers secure can hinder the collaboration AI requires.

The response has been to develop AI-aware container runtimes that understand these unique requirements. NVIDIA's Container Toolkit allows containers to access GPU resources efficiently. MPI operators enable the tightly coupled communication required for distributed training. These aren't just technical improvements—they represent recognition that AI computation has fundamentally different patterns than traditional applications.

The Open Platform for Enterprise AI (OPEA), launched by the Linux Foundation, represents the industry's recognition that AI platforms need standardization and interoperability. OPEA isn't trying to create another platform but to establish common interfaces and practices that allow different AI systems to work together. It addresses a critical challenge: as organizations adopt multiple AI tools and platforms, they risk creating new silos that prevent integrated AI workflows.

OPEA's approach focuses on composability—the ability to combine different AI components into integrated solutions. This reflects a key insight: no single platform will meet all enterprise AI needs. Organizations need to combine specialized tools for computer vision, natural language processing, and predictive analytics. They need to integrate AI services from multiple cloud providers. They need to maintain governance and security across heterogeneous systems.

The standardization efforts extend to crucial areas like model serving, feature stores, and monitoring. Model serving—deploying trained AI models for inference—seems straightforward but involves complex decisions about batching, caching, and version management. Feature stores centralize the preprocessed data features used across multiple models, ensuring consistency and reusability. Monitoring AI systems requires tracking not just traditional metrics like latency and throughput but AI-specific concerns like model drift and fairness.

These enterprise platforms reveal patterns that will likely influence AI-native operating systems. The need for specialized scheduling that understands AI workloads. The importance of seamless transitions between training and inference. The requirement for sophisticated resource sharing that maintains isolation while enabling collaboration. The necessity of capturing and managing the entire context of AI computation, not just the final artifacts.

The platforms also demonstrate the ecosystem effects of AI adoption. NVIDIA's success comes not just from powerful hardware but from comprehensive software stacks, extensive documentation, and vibrant developer communities. Kubernetes succeeded in the AI space not through top-down design but through extensibility that allowed the community to adapt it for machine learning. OPEA recognizes that standards emerge from practice, not prescription.

The evolution of these platforms offers lessons for AI-native operating systems. First, AI workloads are fundamentally different and require purpose-built abstractions. Second, the boundaries between development, training, and deployment blur in AI systems. Third, reproducibility and auditability are essential when systems learn and adapt. Fourth, no single approach will dominate—interoperability and composability are crucial.

As enterprises increasingly rely on AI for critical operations, these platforms become the foundation for digital transformation. They're not just tools for data scientists but infrastructure that must meet enterprise requirements for reliability, security, and governance. The lessons learned from deploying AI at enterprise scale inform the design of operating systems where AI isn't an add-on but the core architecture.

The next chapter explores how these enterprise patterns extend to the edge, where AI must operate in resource-constrained environments without reliable connectivity. The challenges of edge AI—limited power, minimal memory, real-time requirements—push the boundaries of what's possible and point toward innovations that will benefit all AI systems. The future of AI isn't just in massive data centers but in the billions of devices at the edge of our networks.

CHAPTER 12

Edge and IoT Integration

The future of AI isn't in data centers—it's in the trillion devices at the edges of our networks. From industrial sensors monitoring pipeline pressure to cameras watching for wildlife on remote highways, the physical world is becoming instrumented with devices that need intelligence but can't rely on cloud connectivity. This shift toward edge AI represents one of the most challenging and transformative aspects of AI-native operating systems.

The constraints are brutal. A typical edge device might have a few kilobytes of RAM—less memory than a single email. It might run on battery power that needs to last for years. It might operate in environments where temperatures swing from arctic cold to desert heat. Yet we're asking these devices to run neural networks, make intelligent decisions, and participate in distributed AI systems. It seems impossible until you realize that impossibility often precedes innovation.

TinyML—machine learning for microcontrollers—demonstrates what becomes possible when we rethink fundamental assumptions. Traditional machine learning assumes abundant resources: gigabytes of RAM, powerful processors, reliable power. TinyML researchers asked a different question: what if we have 256 kilobytes of memory and need to run on a coin cell battery for two years?

The answers have been remarkable. Researchers have created neural networks that run on devices smaller than a fingernail. These aren't toy demonstrations—they're practical systems performing speech recognition, anomaly detection, and predictive maintenance. A vibration sensor on an industrial motor can learn normal operating patterns and detect developing failures weeks before they cause breakdowns. A wildlife camera can identify specific species and only transmit relevant images, saving bandwidth and power.

The techniques that enable TinyML reveal principles that benefit all AI systems. Quantization reduces neural network weights from 32-bit floating-point to 8-bit or even 1-bit integers, shrinking models by 4x to 32x with minimal accuracy loss. Pruning removes unnecessary connections, sometimes eliminating 90% of parameters while maintaining performance. Knowledge distillation trains small models to mimic large ones, capturing essential behaviors in compact forms.

But TinyML isn't just about shrinking existing models. It requires fundamental rethinking of architectures. Researchers develop neural networks specifically for edge constraints, with architectures that minimize memory access—often the dominant power consumer in edge devices. They create training techniques that produce models optimized for specific hardware. They design inference engines that exploit every capability of minimal processors.

The automotive industry provides a compelling case study in edge AI deployment through AUTOSAR Adaptive. AUTOSAR (AUTomotive Open System ARchitecture) traditionally defined standards for automotive software in a pre-AI world. AUTOSAR Adaptive represents the industry's recognition that modern vehicles are rolling AI platforms that happen to have wheels.

A modern car contains over 100 electronic control units (ECUs), many running AI workloads. Camera systems process video streams for lane detection, pedestrian recognition, and traffic sign reading. Sensor fusion algorithms combine inputs from radar, lidar, and ultrasonic sensors to build environmental models. Path planning systems make real-time decisions about vehicle control. All of this must happen with latencies measured in milliseconds—there's no time to consult the cloud when avoiding a collision.

AUTOSAR Adaptive provides the framework for managing this complexity. It defines how AI components communicate, how they share computational resources, and how they maintain safety guarantees. The platform supports dynamic deployment of software components, allowing vehicles to download and activate new AI models—imagine your car learning to recognize new types of road hazards through over-the-air updates.

The safety requirements in automotive systems push edge AI to its limits. Traditional AI systems can tolerate occasional errors—a misclassified image in a photo app is annoying but not catastrophic. Automotive AI must meet strict safety standards. This drives innovations in redundancy, verification, and fail-safe operation that benefit all edge AI deployments.

The real power of edge AI emerges in distributed intelligence architectures where devices collaborate to solve problems too complex for any single device. Consider a smart building with thousands of sensors monitoring temperature, occupancy, air quality, and energy usage. Each sensor has limited capabilities, but together they form a distributed intelligence that can optimize comfort while minimizing energy consumption.

These architectures challenge traditional notions of hierarchy and control. Instead of sensors sending raw data to a central server for processing, edge devices process data locally and share insights. A temperature sensor doesn't just report readings—it identifies patterns and anomalies. An occupancy sensor doesn't just detect presence—it learns usage patterns and predicts future needs. The intelligence is distributed throughout the network, with no single point of failure.

Distributed intelligence enables new forms of privacy-preserving computation. Instead of sending sensitive data to central servers, edge devices can perform local analysis and share only aggregated insights. A health monitoring device can detect concerning patterns without transmitting raw biometric data. Security cameras can identify threats without storing or transmitting video of innocent bystanders. Privacy becomes an architectural feature, not an afterthought.

The coordination of distributed intelligence requires new approaches to consensus and decision-making. Traditional distributed systems focus on data consistency—ensuring all nodes agree on facts. Distributed AI systems must achieve behavioral consistency—ensuring collective actions align despite individual variations. This might mean multiple edge devices voting on detected events, or negotiating resource allocation without central coordination.

Real-time AI decision making at the edge faces unique challenges. Cloud-based AI can take seconds to process requests—acceptable for many applications but fatal for others. An industrial robot can't wait for cloud responses when avoiding collisions. An autonomous drone can't consult remote servers when navigating obstacles. Edge AI must make decisions in milliseconds with whatever information is locally available.

This drives innovations in incremental and

anytime algorithms. Instead of waiting for complete data, edge AI systems must work with partial information, refining decisions as more data arrives. They must provide useful outputs even if interrupted—a partially planned path is better than no path. They must balance decision quality with timing constraints, sometimes choosing good-enough answers delivered quickly over optimal answers delivered late.

The resource constraints of edge devices create surprising innovations in collaborative processing. Devices can share computational loads, with one device's idle cycles helping another's peak demands. They can distribute model components, with different devices hosting different layers of neural networks. They can implement swarm intelligence, where simple behaviors in many devices create complex collective capabilities.

Power efficiency becomes an obsession in edge AI. Every computation consumes energy, and many edge devices have strict power budgets. This drives research into event-driven processing—computing only when something interesting happens. It motivates approximate computing—accepting slight inaccuracies for significant power savings. It inspires neuromorphic architectures that mimic the brain's efficient information processing.

The integration challenges between edge and cloud AI systems mirror the broader challenges of AI-native operating systems. Edge devices need to operate autonomously when disconnected but collaborate when connected. They must maintain consistency despite intermittent communication. They must balance local optimization with global objectives. These patterns—autonomous operation with collaborative capability—will likely characterize AI-native operating systems at all scales.

The tools and frameworks for edge AI are rapidly maturing. TensorFlow Lite and PyTorch Mobile bring sophisticated machine learning to mobile and embedded devices. Edge Impulse provides integrated workflows for developing and deploying edge AI. ONNX Runtime enables models trained in various frameworks to run efficiently on edge hardware. The ecosystem grows daily, making edge AI accessible to more developers and applications.

As edge AI capabilities expand, we're seeing convergence with enterprise platforms. Kubernetes is extending to edge deployments through projects like K3s and KubeEdge. Cloud providers offer edge computing services that extend their AI platforms to distributed locations. The boundary between edge and cloud blurs as computing becomes truly distributed.

The implications extend beyond technical architecture to fundamental questions about intelligence and autonomy. When billions of devices can sense, think, and act independently, yet coordinate for collective goals, we're creating a form of ambient intelligence that pervades our environment. The operating systems that manage this intelligence must be radically different from those designed for isolated computers.

The next chapter explores how these edge capabilities combine with enterprise platforms to enable new forms of privacy-preserving computation. When intelligence is distributed to the edge, privacy can be protected by design rather than policy. The future of AI isn't just smart—it's inherently private, processing sensitive data where it's generated rather than where it's centralized.

CHAPTER 13

Privacy and Trust

The paradox of AI systems is that they become more helpful the more they know about us, yet every bit of knowledge shared increases our vulnerability. This tension—between capability and privacy—represents one of the defining challenges for AI-native operating systems. The solution isn't to choose between intelligence and privacy but to architect systems where privacy enables rather than constrains AI capabilities.

Traditional approaches to privacy rely on walls and gates. Don't collect sensitive data. If you must collect it, encrypt it in transit and at rest. Limit access through authentication and authorization. Delete it when no longer needed. These approaches made sense when data processing was simple and centralized. But AI systems need to understand patterns across vast amounts of personal data—health records, financial transactions, behavioral patterns, communication networks. The walls-and-gates approach would cripple AI's potential to help us.

Confidential computing represents a fundamental breakthrough in this dilemma. Technologies like Intel's TDX (Trust Domain Extensions) and AMD's SEV-SNP (Secure Encrypted Virtualization-Secure Nested Paging) create secure enclaves where data remains encrypted even during processing. The processor itself becomes the only trusted component, decrypting data within the chip, performing computations, and re-encrypting results before they leave. Even if attackers compromise the operating system, hypervisor, or firmware, they cannot access data within these enclaves.

This isn't theoretical—major cloud providers now offer confidential computing services, and the technology is rapidly expanding. Financial institutions use it to analyze fraud patterns across customer data without exposing individual transactions. Healthcare organizations train diagnostic AI models on patient data without violating privacy regulations. Governments compute statistics on citizen data without accessing individual records. The impossible becomes possible: computation without observation.

The implications for AI-native operating systems are profound. Instead of treating privacy as a constraint on AI capabilities, confidential computing makes privacy an enabler. AI models can train on sensitive data without exposing it. Personal assistants can learn from intimate details of our lives without making us vulnerable. Systems can be both deeply knowledgeable and fundamentally trustworthy.

But confidential computing is just one piece of the privacy puzzle. The choice between on-device and cloud processing represents a fundamental architectural decision with cascading implications. On-device processing keeps data local—your photos never leave your phone, your documents never leave your laptop. Cloud processing offers virtually unlimited computational power and the ability to learn from aggregated patterns across many users. The trade-offs seem stark until you realize they're not binary choices.

On-device processing has matured remarkably. Modern smartphones contain neural processing units capable of running sophisticated AI models. Laptops can perform complex natural language processing without network connectivity. Edge devices can make intelligent decisions with minimal hardware. The capability gap between local and cloud processing shrinks daily, making on-device AI increasingly viable for sensitive applications.

The advantages extend beyond privacy. On-device processing eliminates network latency, enabling real-time applications impossible with cloud processing. It works offline, crucial for mobile devices and remote locations. It reduces bandwidth consumption and cloud computing costs. It distributes computational load, improving system scalability. Privacy becomes a beneficial side effect of good architecture.

Yet cloud processing offers unique advantages that on-device processing cannot match. Training large language models requires computational resources no personal device possesses. Learning from patterns across millions of users enables capabilities impossible with individual data. Continuous model updates based on emerging threats or opportunities require centralized coordination. The cloud enables collective intelligence that benefits everyone.

The solution emerges in hybrid architectures that intelligently balance on-device and cloud processing. Personal data processing happens locally—your AI assistant learns your writing style on your device. Pattern learning happens in the cloud—aggregated and anonymized insights improve everyone's experience. Sensitive operations stay local while non-sensitive operations leverage cloud resources. The architecture adapts to context, regulations, and user preferences.

User data sovereignty—the principle that individuals should control their own data—becomes architectural reality in AI-native operating systems. Traditional systems treat user data as something to be collected, processed, and monetized. AI-native systems recognize data as remaining fundamentally owned by users, with systems granted specific permissions for specific purposes.

This sovereignty manifests in concrete capabilities. Users can see exactly what data AI systems have learned about them—not raw data dumps but meaningful insights. They can correct misconceptions, delete specific knowledge, or reset entire learning histories. They can grant granular permissions—allow health pattern learning but not financial analysis. They can export their AI's knowledge when switching systems, maintaining continuity of personalization.

The technical challenges are significant. How do you delete specific knowledge from a neural network that distributes information across millions of parameters? How do you explain what an AI has learned in terms users understand? How do you enable data portability between systems with different architectures? These challenges drive innovations in interpretable AI, selective forgetting, and standardized knowledge representations.

Regulatory compliance adds another layer of complexity. GDPR in Europe, CCPA in California, and emerging regulations worldwide establish strict requirements for data handling. AI systems must not only comply but demonstrate compliance—proving they've deleted data when requested, showing they're not using data for unauthorized purposes, documenting their decision-making processes. Traditional compliance approaches—auditing databases and reviewing access logs—fail when dealing with neural networks and distributed learning.

AI-native operating systems must build compliance into their architecture. Privacy-by-design principles mean considering privacy implications at every architectural decision. Data minimization ensures systems learn what they need without storing unnecessary details. Purpose limitation prevents mission creep where data collected for one purpose gets used for another. These aren't features added after the fact but fundamental design constraints.

The emergence of privacy-enhancing technologies creates new possibilities. Differential privacy adds carefully calibrated noise to data, preserving statistical patterns while protecting individuals. Homomorphic encryption enables computation on encrypted data without decryption. Secure multi-party computation allows multiple parties to jointly compute functions while keeping inputs private. These technologies, once academic curiosities, now enable practical privacy-preserving AI systems.

Federated learning exemplifies how privacy can enhance rather than hinder AI capabilities. Instead of centralizing data for training, federated learning brings training to data. Devices train models locally and share only model updates—mathematical gradients that reveal patterns but not specifics. A keyboard app can learn typing patterns across millions of users without seeing what anyone types. A health app can identify disease patterns without accessing individual health records.

The trust implications extend beyond technical architecture to user experience. AI-native operating systems must make privacy comprehensible and controllable. Users need dashboards showing what their system knows and why. They need simple controls for common privacy preferences and detailed controls for specific concerns. They need confidence that saying "forget this" actually means forgetting, not just hiding.

Building trust requires transparency about capabilities and limitations. When AI systems make decisions affecting users, they must explain their reasoning in understandable terms. When they share data for collective benefit, they must clearly communicate what's shared and why. When breaches or errors occur, they must promptly notify affected users. Trust builds slowly through consistent behavior and erodes quickly through violations.

The business models of AI-native operating systems must align with privacy principles. Traditional platforms monetize user data through targeted advertising and behavioral analytics. Privacy-respecting systems need alternative models —subscriptions, computational fees, value-added services. The economics must support privacy rather than undermine it.

International variations in privacy expectations and regulations create additional challenges. What's acceptable in one culture may be invasive in another. Systems must adapt to local requirements while maintaining global interoperability. They must respect the strictest applicable regulations while remaining usable everywhere. This drives architectures that treat privacy as configurable rather than fixed.

The next chapter explores the practical implications of these privacy-preserving architectures for productivity and work. When AI systems can be both highly capable and deeply private, they enable new forms of collaboration and creativity. The future of work isn't just augmented by AI—it's transformed by AI we can trust.

CHAPTER 14

Reimagining Productivity

The modern knowledge worker spends nearly 20% of their time simply looking for information. Another 20% goes to repetitive tasks that haven't changed in decades—copying data between applications, reformatting documents, scheduling meetings. We've built incredibly powerful computers, then shackled them with workflows that treat them as glorified typewriters. AI-native operating systems promise to shatter these chains, transforming not just how fast we work, but how we work at all.

Consider a typical Monday morning. You arrive to find 147 emails, 12 meeting requests, and 6 urgent messages across 3 different platforms. Your task list spans 4 applications. The presentation due Wednesday needs data from spreadsheets last updated Friday, charts from a tool you haven't opened in weeks, and compliance text from a document you can't quite remember the name of. By the time you've gathered everything, half the morning is gone—spent not on creative work but on digital archaeology.

This isn't a failure of individual applications. Email clients have become sophisticated. Spreadsheet software can perform miracles of calculation. Presentation tools create stunning visuals. The failure is systemic—each application is an island, forcing us to be the bridges between them. We've digitized work without fundamentally reimagining it.

Intelligent automation in AI-native operating systems doesn't just speed up these bridges—it eliminates them. When you start working on that presentation, the system already knows what you need. It has observed that presentations to the board always include quarterly metrics, competitive analysis, and forward projections. It has learned that you prefer specific chart styles for financial data and different ones for market trends. It understands the relationships between your various documents.

The automation goes beyond simple templates or macros. As you begin outlining your presentation, the system is already gathering relevant data. It notices you're working on Q3 results and automatically pulls the latest figures from your financial systems. It sees you mention competitive positioning and assembles recent market intelligence. It recognizes compliance requirements for board communications and suggests appropriate disclaimers. This isn't rule-based automation—it's intelligent assistance based on understanding context and intent.

The system learns from every interaction. When you reject a suggested chart, it understands not just that you didn't want that specific visualization but why—perhaps the scale was misleading or the color scheme didn't match your theme. When you rephrase suggested text, it learns your communication style. When you add data sources it hadn't considered, it expands its understanding of what's relevant for similar tasks. The automation becomes more helpful over time, not through programming but through partnership.

This intelligent automation extends to workflows that span multiple applications and people. Consider expense reporting—a task universally despised for its tedium. In current systems, you photograph receipts, manually enter data, categorize expenses, attach documentation, route for approval, and respond to questions. Each step involves different applications, redundant data entry, and opportunities for error.

In an AI-native system, the workflow transforms completely. Photograph a receipt, and the system extracts all relevant information, matches it to calendar events to understand context, categorizes it based on learned patterns, and prepares the expense report automatically. It knows that dinner with certain contacts is business development, that taxi rides between specific locations relate to client visits, that recurring subscriptions need different documentation. When anomalies arise—an unusually large expense or a new category—it asks clarifying questions rather than guessing.

But the real transformation comes from context-aware assistance that understands not just individual tasks but your entire work context. The system knows you're preparing for a product launch. It sees the interconnected activities—development milestones, marketing campaigns, sales enablement, customer communications. It understands how delays in one area cascade to others. It can proactively identify risks and suggest mitigations.

This contextual awareness manifests in countless small but powerful ways. When you're writing an email about project status, the system knows which metrics are relevant and can insert current values automatically. When you're scheduling a meeting, it understands the participants' roles and suggests appropriate durations and agendas. When you're reviewing a contract, it highlights clauses that differ from your standard terms. The assistance feels less like using tools and more like having a knowledgeable colleague who never forgets anything.

The context spans time as well as space. The system remembers that six months ago you dealt with a similar challenge and can surface relevant documents and decisions. It knows that certain types of requests tend to arrive at month-end and can prepare resources in advance. It learns seasonal patterns in your work and adjusts its assistance accordingly. Your digital workspace has memory that enhances rather than burdens.

Predictive application behavior takes this further by anticipating needs before they're expressed. Traditional applications wait for commands—open when clicked, compute when instructed, save when told. AI-native applications predict and prepare. They pre-load components you're likely to need. They begin calculations before you ask. They draft responses while you're still reading requests.

This prediction isn't just about speed—it's about cognitive flow. The biggest productivity killer isn't slow software but interrupted thinking. Every time you stop to search for information, wait for an application to load, or figure out how to accomplish a task, your mental context evaporates. Predictive systems maintain your flow by ensuring what you need is ready when you need it.

The predictions become remarkably sophisticated. The system might notice that when you open certain financial models on Monday mornings, you typically update them with weekend trading data. It can fetch that data and prepare update scenarios before you arrive. It might observe that design review meetings often lead to specification updates and have the relevant documents ready to edit. It might learn that emails from certain clients require consulting specific contracts and surface them automatically.

But perhaps the most transformative aspect is the end of application silos. Current operating systems treat applications as sovereign territories with rigid borders. Data lives in specific applications.

Capabilities are trapped within individual programs. Moving information or functionality between applications requires explicit export and import operations, often losing context and capabilities in translation.

AI-native operating systems dissolve these boundaries. Capabilities flow to where they're needed. When you're writing a document and need to create a chart, visualization capabilities appear inline—you don't "switch to" a charting application. When you're in a video call and need to analyze data, computational capabilities manifest naturally—you don't "share your screen" from another application. The system presents unified capabilities rather than fragmented applications.

This dissolution of silos enables workflows impossible today. Imagine analyzing customer feedback that arrives through email, support tickets, social media, and phone transcripts. Current systems would require exporting from each source, importing to analysis tools, manually aligning formats, and building visualizations separately. In an AI-native system, analysis capabilities flow across all data sources. Sentiment analysis, theme extraction, and trend visualization happen holistically, regardless of where data originated.

The unified workspace extends to collaboration. When working with colleagues, you don't "share documents"—you share contexts. Others can see not just the final artifact but the thinking behind it, the data sources used, the alternatives considered. They can build on your work without recreating your research. They can understand decisions without lengthy explanations. Collaboration becomes cumulative rather than repetitive.

This transformation faces real challenges. Privacy and security become more complex when capabilities flow freely. How do you ensure that the chart created from financial data doesn't retain sensitive information when moved to a public presentation? How do you maintain audit trails when transformations happen fluidly? How do you prevent capability flow from becoming a security vulnerability?

User control and transparency are essential. While the system can automate and predict, users must retain agency. Every automation needs an override. Every prediction needs an alternative. Every flowing capability needs clear boundaries. The system must be helpful without being presumptuous, intelligent without being opaque.

The learning curve presents another challenge. Users trained on application-centric workflows need to adapt to capability-centric thinking. The mental model shifts from "what application do I need?" to "what am I trying to accomplish?" This is ultimately liberating but initially disorienting. The transition requires thoughtful design and patient support.

Yet the productivity gains justify the effort. Studies of early AI-native systems show dramatic improvements—not just in speed but in quality.

When workers spend less time on mechanical tasks, they have more energy for creative thinking. When systems handle routine coordination, humans can focus on strategic decisions. When information flows naturally, insights emerge that were previously hidden in silos.

The next chapter explores how this productivity transformation becomes deeply personal through AI systems that adapt to individual work styles and preferences. When operating systems truly understand how each person works best, they can create environments optimized for individual flourishing. The future of productivity isn't just intelligent—it's intimately personalized.

CHAPTER 15

Personalization and Adaptation

Every morning, millions of people sit down at computers configured exactly the same way they were yesterday, last month, and last year. The interface shows no recognition of who's using it, what they're trying to accomplish, or how they prefer to work. It's as if your office rearranged itself randomly each night, forcing you to hunt for tools and reorganize your workspace before beginning actual work. We've accepted this digital amnesia for so long that we barely notice the friction it creates.

The promise of AI-native operating systems isn't just intelligence—it's personal intelligence. Systems that learn not just general patterns but your specific patterns. Interfaces that adapt not to some abstract average user but to you. Computing environments that evolve with your skills, accommodate your preferences, and amplify your unique strengths. This isn't customization through settings menus—it's continuous adaptation through understanding.

Learning individual usage patterns begins the moment you start using an AI-native system, but not in the creepy, surveillance-capitalism way we've grown to fear. The system observes how you work to serve you better, not to serve advertisers. It notices that you prefer keyboard shortcuts to mouse clicks, that you work in focused bursts rather than continuous sessions, that you organize information spatially rather than hierarchically. These observations build a model of your work style that influences every interaction.

The patterns go deeper than surface preferences. The system learns your cognitive rhythms—when you're most creative, when you prefer routine tasks, when you need breaks. It understands your communication patterns—formal with clients, casual with teammates, technical with developers. It recognizes your decision-making style—whether you prefer complete information before acting or iterate through rapid experiments. This isn't psychoanalysis—it's practical observation aimed at reducing friction.

Traditional personalization asks users to configure preferences through endless settings panels. Do you want notifications? Which ones? When? How? With what sound? The combinatorial explosion of options becomes overwhelming, so most users stick with defaults that serve no one well. AI-native personalization learns through observation, adjusting automatically while allowing explicit overrides when needed.

Consider how this transforms something as simple as notifications. Current systems bombard us with interruptions or force us to silence everything, missing critical alerts. An AI-native system learns which notifications matter to you and when. It notices that you immediately respond to messages from certain people but ignore others until natural breaks. It observes that calendar reminders need different lead times for different meeting types. It understands that "urgent" means different things from different senders. The notification system becomes a intelligent filter, not a fire hose or a wall.

Adaptive user interfaces take personalization from behavior to presentation. Current interfaces are frozen in design decisions made by people who never met you. Button sizes, menu organizations, and tool layouts reflect average users who don't exist. Power users navigate through interfaces cluttered with features they never use. Novices face walls of options they don't understand. Everyone suffers from designs that fit no one.

AI-native interfaces reshape themselves based on your usage. Frequently used functions migrate to prominent positions. Rarely used options fade to the background but remain accessible. Complex features reveal themselves gradually as your expertise grows. The interface becomes a living environment that evolves with your capabilities rather than a static maze you must memorize.

This adaptation goes beyond moving buttons around. The system learns your conceptual models and adjusts its presentation accordingly. If you think of projects in terms of timelines, it emphasizes temporal views. If you organize by relationships, it highlights connections. If you're visual, it prioritizes graphical representations. If you're textual, it focuses on written descriptions. The interface doesn't just rearrange—it translates between the system's capabilities and your mental models.

The adaptation extends to interaction modalities. Some people think by writing, others by speaking, others by sketching. Current systems force everyone into the same interaction patterns. AI-native systems fluidly adjust, letting you sketch ideas that become structured documents, speak thoughts that become written plans, or type commands that become visual workflows. The boundary between input and output blurs as the system translates between your preferred expression and required formats.

Anticipatory computing represents the next level of personalization—systems that prepare for your needs before you express them. This isn't the annoying "It looks like you're writing a letter" assistance of the past. It's subtle, context-aware preparation that removes friction without imposing assumptions. The system doesn't interrupt to offer help—it ensures help is available when needed.

Anticipation manifests in countless ways. Documents you'll need for your morning meeting are cached and indexed before you arrive. Applications update overnight so you never see progress bars during work. Complex calculations begin when you open related files, completing by the time you need results. Resources allocate based on predicted needs rather than reactive demands. The system prepares your digital environment like a skilled assistant preparing a physical workspace.

The anticipation extends to problem prevention. The system notices patterns that precede problems—perhaps certain workflow combinations lead to errors, or specific scheduling patterns create conflicts. It can intervene subtly, suggesting alternatives or preparing safeguards. When you're about to make a mistake you've made before, it offers gentle warnings. When you're entering a situation similar to past challenges, it surfaces relevant solutions. The assistance feels less like a nanny and more like accumulated wisdom.

But anticipatory computing truly shines in creative and complex work. The system learns your creative patterns—how you brainstorm, develop ideas, and refine solutions. When you begin a new project, it can suggest relevant resources from past work, identify potential collaborators with complementary skills, and prepare tools you typically use for similar challenges. It's like having perfect recall of everything you've ever done, organized by relevance to current tasks.

The OS that knows you represents the culmination of these capabilities—a system that understands you as well as a long-time colleague. This knowledge isn't stored as a creepy dossier but embedded in the system's responses and adaptations. It knows you hate redundant data entry, so it eliminates it. It knows you process information visually, so it emphasizes graphics. It knows you work best with background music, so it manages audio automatically.

This deep personalization enables experiences impossible with generic systems. When you're learning new skills, the system adapts its teaching to your learning style—more examples for experiential learners, more theory for conceptual learners, more practice for kinesthetic learners. When you're solving problems, it presents information in formats that match your cognitive style. When you're communicating, it helps translate your thoughts into forms others understand while preserving your voice.

The personalization becomes particularly powerful in collaborative contexts. The system can mediate between different work styles, translating concepts between team members' preferred representations. It can identify when miscommunication stems from different mental models and bridge the gap. It can even suggest optimal team compositions based on complementary cognitive styles and work patterns. Collaboration improves not by forcing everyone into the same mold but by celebrating and bridging differences.

Privacy and control remain paramount in these deeply personalized systems. Users must own their behavioral models and control how they're used. The system must forget when asked, adjust when corrected, and respect boundaries always. Personalization profiles must be portable between systems and deletable on demand. The power of personalization must never become a prison of prediction.

The technical challenges are substantial. Building models that capture individual nuance without overfitting to noise. Adapting interfaces without disorienting users. Anticipating needs without constraining possibilities. Maintaining performance while continuously learning. Protecting privacy while enabling personalization. These aren't just technical problems but design challenges requiring deep understanding of human psychology and behavior.

Yet the benefits transform computing from tool use to partnership. When systems truly understand individual users, technology disappears into the background. The cognitive load of managing computers evaporates. The friction of translation between human intent and machine capability vanishes. We stop adapting to our tools and they start adapting to us.

The implications extend beyond productivity to accessibility and inclusion. Current systems assume standard abilities and preferences, marginalizing users who differ from the norm. AI-native personalization can adapt to any user's capabilities and constraints. Visual interfaces for those who see, auditory for those who hear, tactile for those who touch. Complexity that matches capability. Pace that matches preference. Computing becomes truly personal, and therefore truly universal.

The next chapter explores how this personalized intelligence enables new forms of collaboration. When systems understand individuals deeply, they can facilitate connections and collaborations that amplify collective intelligence. The future isn't just about personal productivity—it's about connecting personalized systems in ways that create emergent capabilities beyond any individual's reach.

CHAPTER 16

Collaborative Intelligence

The most complex challenges facing humanity —climate change, disease, economic inequality—cannot be solved by individual brilliance. They require collective intelligence that combines diverse perspectives, specialized expertise, and coordinated action. Yet our current tools for collaboration are barely evolved from email and shared documents. AI-native operating systems promise something revolutionary: computing environments where collective intelligence emerges naturally from the interaction of human and artificial agents working toward common goals.

Traditional collaboration tools focus on sharing —documents, screens, messages. They're digital versions of passing papers around a conference table. But real collaboration isn't about sharing artifacts; it's about combining capabilities. It's the difference between musicians exchanging sheet music and musicians playing together in harmony. AI-native operating systems enable the latter, creating environments where different forms of intelligence combine and amplify each other.

Multi-agent systems at the OS level transform computers from single-threaded servants to orchestras of specialized capabilities. Instead of one monolithic AI trying to handle everything, specialized agents focus on specific domains. A language agent understands natural communication. A visual agent processes images and spatial relationships. A reasoning agent handles logic and planning. A memory agent maintains context and history. These aren't separate applications but integrated capabilities that work together seamlessly.

The coordination between agents happens through sophisticated protocols that go far beyond traditional inter-process communication. Agents share not just data but understanding. When the visual agent identifies objects in an image, it doesn't just pass labels to other agents—it shares semantic understanding, spatial relationships, and confidence levels. When the reasoning agent develops a plan, it communicates not just steps but assumptions, dependencies, and alternatives. The communication is rich, nuanced, and contextual.

This multi-agent architecture enables capabilities impossible with monolithic systems. Consider debugging complex software. A code analysis agent understands program structure. A behavior agent recognizes execution patterns.

A history agent tracks changes over time. A communication agent interfaces with the developer. Working together, they can identify subtle bugs that would escape any single analysis. The code agent might notice an unusual pattern, the behavior agent confirms it causes problems under specific conditions, the history agent traces when it was introduced, and the communication agent explains the issue in terms the developer understands.

The agents learn to work together over time, developing what might be called collaborative intuition. They discover which agent is best suited for different aspects of problems. They learn when to defer to each other's expertise. They develop shorthand communications that speed coordination. Like a experienced team, they become more effective through practice, but unlike human teams, they never forget lessons learned or suffer from interpersonal friction.

Distributed problem solving takes this collaboration beyond single machines to networks of systems working together. Complex problems naturally decompose into subproblems that different systems can tackle simultaneously. But unlike traditional distributed computing that splits computational tasks, AI-native distribution splits cognitive tasks. Different systems bring different capabilities, perspectives, and resources to bear on shared challenges.

Consider architectural design for a new hospital. The challenge involves medical workflow optimization, building codes, energy efficiency, patient experience, and countless other factors. In an AI-native environment, specialized systems collaborate: medical AI that understands treatment patterns, architectural AI that knows building design, engineering AI that optimizes systems, and regulatory AI that ensures compliance. But they don't work in isolation—they continuously negotiate trade-offs, explore alternatives, and refine solutions together.

The distribution isn't just functional but perspective-based. Different AI systems trained on different data bring diverse viewpoints. An AI trained on European hospitals might emphasize different priorities than one trained on Asian facilities. An AI focused on patient outcomes might conflict with one optimizing operational efficiency. These diverse perspectives, managed through collaborative protocols, lead to solutions that no single perspective would generate. It's cognitive diversity at machine scale.

Human-AI collaboration patterns in these systems go far beyond current "AI assistant" models. Humans and AI agents become true collaborators with complementary strengths. Humans bring creativity, values, and contextual understanding. AI brings processing power, perfect memory, and pattern recognition. But the collaboration patterns are as varied as human relationships themselves.

Sometimes the human leads and AI supports—the human architect sketches concepts while AI agents handle technical details, code compliance, and optimization. Sometimes AI leads and humans guide—AI systems generate therapeutic options while human doctors provide judgment and empathy. Sometimes they work as peers—human researchers and AI systems exploring hypotheses together, each contributing insights the other might miss.

The collaboration becomes fluid and contextual. During brainstorming, AI agents might act as provocateurs, suggesting wild possibilities to spark creativity. During implementation, they become meticulous assistants, catching errors and maintaining consistency. During review, they act as critics, identifying weaknesses and suggesting improvements. The role shifts based on the task, the human's needs, and the stage of work.

These collaboration patterns extend to human-human interaction mediated by AI. When team members have different expertise levels, AI can translate between them—explaining technical details to managers in business terms, or conveying strategic vision to engineers in implementation specifics. When collaborators speak different languages, AI provides not just translation but cultural bridging. When time zones separate team members, AI maintains context and continuity, ensuring no one misses critical developments.

The emergence of collective intelligence from these interactions represents something genuinely new in human experience. It's not just pooled intelligence where capabilities add together. It's emergent intelligence where the interaction creates capabilities that didn't exist in any component. Like consciousness emerging from neurons, collective intelligence emerges from the interplay of human and artificial agents.

This emergence manifests in concrete ways. Research teams discover connections no member saw individually. Design teams create solutions that synthesize perspectives in novel ways. Analysis teams identify patterns that require multiple viewpoints to perceive. The collective develops its own memory, its own problem-solving approaches, its own creative style. It becomes an entity greater than its components.

The collective intelligence adapts and evolves. As teams work together, the AI agents learn not just individual preferences but group dynamics. They understand that certain combinations of people produce creative breakthroughs while others excel at execution. They learn when the group needs convergent thinking versus divergent exploration. They can even identify when the collective is falling into groupthink and introduce productive disruption.

Scale amplifies these effects. When hundreds or thousands of humans collaborate through AI mediation, the collective intelligence can tackle challenges of unprecedented complexity. Climate modeling that incorporates local knowledge from thousands of regions. Medical research that synthesizes insights from every documented case. Economic planning that considers impacts across all affected communities. The AI doesn't replace human judgment—it enables human judgment to operate at previously impossible scales.

The challenges of collaborative intelligence are as significant as its promise. How do you maintain coherence when thousands of agents interact? How do you resolve conflicts between different AI recommendations? How do you ensure human agency isn't lost in the collective? How do you prevent cascade failures where errors propagate through the network? These aren't just technical challenges but fundamental questions about the nature of intelligence and agency.

Governance becomes crucial. Who decides when collective intelligence overrides individual judgment? How do you audit decisions that emerge from complex interactions? How do you assign responsibility when no single agent made the choice? These questions will require new frameworks that go beyond traditional notions of accountability and control.

Yet the potential justifies grappling with these challenges. We're seeing the emergence of a new form of intelligence that combines the best of human and artificial capabilities. Not replacement but augmentation. Not automation but collaboration. Not artificial general intelligence but collective hybrid intelligence that remains fundamentally human-centered while transcending human limitations.

The next chapter explores the technical challenges that must be overcome to realize this vision. From latency and reliability to backward compatibility and standardization, the path to AI-native operating systems requires solving problems that span hardware, software, and human factors. The journey is complex, but the destination—truly intelligent computing environments—justifies the effort.

CHAPTER 17

Technical Challenges

The vision of AI-native operating systems is compelling, but the path from vision to reality runs through a minefield of technical challenges. Each breakthrough described in previous chapters—from natural language interfaces to collaborative intelligence—depends on solving problems that push the boundaries of current technology. These aren't mere implementation details; they're fundamental obstacles that will determine whether AI-native operating systems remain an interesting concept or become the foundation of future computing.

Latency might seem like a solved problem in an era of gigahertz processors and fiber optic networks. But AI-native operating systems face latency challenges that make traditional optimization seem trivial. When every interaction involves neural network inference, when natural language must be processed in real-time, when multiple AI agents must coordinate responses, milliseconds matter in ways they never have before.

Consider what happens when you speak to an AI-native system. Your voice must be captured, processed into digital signals, converted to text, parsed for meaning, routed to appropriate agents, processed through potentially multiple neural networks, formulated into responses, and converted back to speech or action. Each step involves complex computation. In traditional systems, you click a button and trigger a predetermined function. In AI systems, you speak a request and trigger a cascade of intelligent processing.

The challenge compounds when real-time requirements meet AI uncertainty. A traditional operating system can guarantee that pressing the brake pedal in a car will engage brakes within a specific timeframe. Every step is deterministic and bounded. But when an AI system must interpret sensor data, understand the situation, and decide on actions, how do you guarantee response times? The neural network might need more inference cycles for complex scenes. The language model might generate longer responses for nuanced requests. The very flexibility that makes AI powerful makes it unpredictable.

Current solutions involve fascinating trade-offs. Some systems run multiple models simultaneously—a fast, simple model provides immediate responses while a complex model refines them. Others use predictive processing, beginning computations before they're needed based on context. Still others implement "anytime algorithms" that provide increasingly accurate results over time, allowing systems to respond quickly with rough answers while continuing to refine them.

Hardware acceleration helps but isn't a complete solution. Neural processing units can speed inference by orders of magnitude, but they introduce their own latencies—data must be formatted, transferred, processed, and returned. The coordination overhead can eliminate the acceleration benefits for small models or simple queries. It's like having a sports car in city traffic—theoretical speed doesn't translate to practical performance.

Energy efficiency considerations add another dimension to these challenges. Traditional computers are already power-hungry, but AI workloads can be voracious. Training large language models requires megawatts of power. Even inference—just running trained models—consumes significant energy. When every interaction involves AI processing, power consumption could skyrocket, making devices unusable on battery power and data centers unsustainable.

The problem is fundamental to how neural networks compute. Traditional processors can skip unnecessary calculations, shut down unused circuits, and optimize for minimal work. Neural networks must process every connection, every weight, every activation. A traditional search might examine a few database entries. An AI search might process millions of parameters. The computational requirements are orders of magnitude different.

Innovation in this space is rapid and multifaceted. Researchers develop sparse models where most connections are zero, reducing computation without sacrificing accuracy. Hardware designers create processors that can skip zero operations entirely. Algorithm designers find ways to compress models, quantize weights, and distill knowledge into smaller networks. But each optimization involves trade-offs between efficiency and capability.

The energy challenge extends beyond individual devices to systemic concerns. If every computer becomes an AI computer, if every interaction involves neural processing, the global energy impact could be enormous. Data centers already consume percent-scale global electricity. AI-native operating systems could multiply this consumption unless efficiency improves dramatically. It's not just a technical challenge but an environmental imperative.

Backward compatibility presents a different but equally critical challenge. The world runs on decades of accumulated software. Millions of applications, billions of documents, trillions of files exist in current formats. AI-native operating systems can't simply declare this legacy obsolete. They must bridge between the old and new worlds while enabling the transformative capabilities that justify their existence.

The challenge goes beyond file formats and APIs. Current software embodies assumptions about how computers work—deterministic execution, explicit commands, static interfaces. How does legacy software run in a probabilistic environment? How do applications designed for keyboard and mouse work with natural language interfaces? How do programs that expect file systems find data in semantic storage?

Virtualization offers one approach—run legacy environments within AI-native systems. But this creates islands of old-style computing within new paradigms, limiting integration and benefits. Translation offers another approach—adapt legacy interfaces to new capabilities. But this risks lowest-common-denominator solutions that sacrifice innovation for compatibility.

The most promising approaches involve gradual transformation. Legacy applications gain AI capabilities through system services—natural language interfaces that translate to traditional commands, semantic search that maps to file operations, intelligent automation that scripts existing functions. Over time, applications can adopt native capabilities while maintaining familiar operations. It's evolution, not revolution, but evolution guided by a revolutionary vision.

Standardization needs become critical as AI-native systems proliferate. Without standards, we risk fragmenting into incompatible islands of intelligence. Models trained for one system won't run on another. Natural language interfaces will interpret commands differently. Collaborative agents won't be able to communicate across platforms. The tower of Babel rebuilt in silicon and code.

Yet standardization faces unique challenges in AI systems. Traditional standards define precise behaviors—this function returns that value. AI systems are inherently probabilistic—responses vary, behaviors adapt, capabilities evolve. How do you standardize systems designed to learn and change? How do you ensure interoperability between systems that might develop different understandings?

The standardization challenge extends to evaluation and certification. How do you verify an AI-native operating system works correctly when "correctly" includes probabilistic behavior? How do you certify safety-critical systems when responses might vary? How do you audit systems that learn and change after deployment? Traditional testing assumes deterministic behavior that AI systems deliberately avoid.

Current efforts focus on standardizing interfaces rather than implementations. Define how agents communicate without specifying how they think. Establish protocols for capability discovery without mandating specific capabilities. Create frameworks for privacy and security without constraining innovation. It's a delicate balance between enabling interoperability and preserving flexibility.

The interaction between these technical

challenges creates compound difficulties. Real-time requirements conflict with energy efficiency—faster responses require more power. Backward compatibility conflicts with innovation—supporting legacy constrains new designs. Standardization conflicts with experimentation—premature standards can freeze immature designs. Solving any one challenge often exacerbates others.

Yet solutions emerge from unexpected directions. Neuromorphic computing promises orders-of-magnitude efficiency improvements by mimicking brain architectures. Quantum computing might accelerate certain AI operations beyond classical limits. New materials and manufacturing processes enable chips optimized for AI workloads. The same creativity that envisions AI-native operating systems drives innovations to realize them.

The technical challenges are real and significant, but they're not insurmountable. Every computing revolution faced similar obstacles. Moving from mainframes to personal computers seemed impossible until microprocessors emerged. Connecting computers globally seemed impractical until internet protocols standardized. Making computers mobile seemed unfeasible until battery and wireless technologies matured. Each transformation required solving problems that seemed fundamental barriers until they weren't.

The difference with AI-native operating systems is that we're not just optimizing existing paradigms but creating new ones. We're not just making computers faster but making them think. We're not just improving interfaces but enabling understanding. We're not just connecting systems but creating collective intelligence. The technical challenges reflect the ambition of the transformation.

The next chapter explores the social and ethical implications of solving these technical challenges. When we create operating systems that understand language, learn from behavior, and collaborate with humans, we're not just engineering software—we're designing relationships between humans and machines that will shape society for generations. The technical challenges are difficult, but the social challenges may be even more profound.

CHAPTER 18

Social and Ethical Implications

The most profound technologies are often the most invisible. Electricity transformed society not when power plants were built, but when electric light became so common we stopped noticing it. The internet changed everything not with the first network connections, but when being online became as natural as breathing. AI-native operating systems promise a similar transformation—computing so intelligent and intuitive that it disappears into the fabric of daily life. But this very invisibility raises urgent questions about who benefits, who controls, and who understands these systems that will mediate so much of human experience.

The digital divide has been with us since the first personal computers, but AI-native operating systems threaten to transform it from a gap into a chasm. Traditional computers require literacy and basic technical skills. AI-native systems require something more subtle but potentially more exclusionary: the ability to communicate intent, to understand probabilistic responses, and to maintain agency in partnership with intelligent systems. Those who master this new form of literacy will have unprecedented capabilities at their command. Those who don't risk becoming digital serfs in their own society.

Consider the economic implications. Current computers are tools—powerful but passive. Anyone with basic skills can use them equally. But AI-native systems learn and adapt to their users. A system used by an expert becomes more expert. One used by a professional in a specific field becomes specialized in that domain. Over time, the gap between a well-trained AI system and a basic one could become insurmountable. We risk creating a world where the rich don't just have better computers—they have computers that know more, can do more, and enable more.

The geographic dimension compounds this concern. AI-native systems require significant computational resources, reliable connectivity, and continuous updates. Regions with robust infrastructure will have systems that learn from millions of users, accessing vast knowledge bases and collaborative networks. Isolated areas might have systems running in degraded modes, learning slowly if at all. The same technology that could democratize access to intelligence might instead concentrate it in already-privileged areas.

Yet the potential for positive transformation is equally real. Natural language interfaces could make computing accessible to billions who struggle with traditional interfaces. People who speak minority languages, who lack formal education, or who think differently could find AI systems that adapt to them rather than forcing adaptation. The same flexibility that creates risks also creates opportunities for inclusion never before possible.

Accessibility in AI interfaces represents both the greatest promise and the greatest challenge of these systems. Traditional accessibility tools are add-ons—screen readers for the blind, voice controls for those who can't use keyboards, simplified interfaces for cognitive differences. They work, but they're clearly accommodations, often providing degraded experiences. AI-native systems could transform accessibility from accommodation to adaptation.

Imagine systems that don't just read screens to blind users but understand content and context, providing rich descriptions and intelligent navigation. Systems that don't just accept voice commands but understand the speech patterns of users with motor disabilities, learning and adapting to their specific needs. Systems that recognize cognitive differences and adjust complexity, pacing, and presentation accordingly. Accessibility becomes not a special mode but the natural result of systems that adapt to all users.

But this promise depends on design decisions made now. If AI systems train primarily on data from typical users, they may struggle with atypical patterns. If natural language processing focuses on standard speech, it may exclude those with speech differences. If interfaces optimize for efficiency over understanding, they may become inaccessible to those who need more time or different approaches. The choices made in developing AI-native systems will determine whether they become tools of inclusion or exclusion.

The challenge extends beyond individual accessibility to cognitive accessibility. Current computers are ultimately comprehensible—with enough study, you can understand how they work. But neural networks are opaque even to their creators. When an AI system makes a decision, it often can't explain why in terms humans understand. This opacity becomes critical when these systems make decisions affecting our lives—what information we see, what opportunities we're offered, what access we're granted.

Bias in OS-level decision making represents one of the most insidious risks of AI-native systems. Every AI system reflects the biases in its training data and design choices. But when bias exists in an application, you can choose another. When it exists in the operating system itself, it affects everything you do. A biased scheduling algorithm might systematically disadvantage certain types of tasks. A biased resource allocator might provide fewer capabilities to certain users. A biased interface might make some activities harder than others based on hidden assumptions.

These biases can be subtle and cumulative. An AI system trained primarily on data from one culture might misunderstand requests from another. One optimized for certain work patterns might penalize different approaches. One that learns from biased human behavior might amplify those biases. Over time, small biases compound into systematic disadvantages, all hidden beneath interfaces that seem neutral and helpful.

The invisibility of these biases makes them particularly dangerous. When a human shows bias, we can recognize and address it. When an AI system shows bias, it often appears as objective computation. The system doesn't say "I'm giving you fewer resources because of bias"—it just allocates resources according to opaque algorithms. Users experience the effects without understanding the causes, often blaming themselves rather than recognizing systematic bias.

Addressing bias requires more than technical solutions. It demands diverse teams building these systems, comprehensive testing across different populations, and continuous monitoring for emergent biases. It requires transparency about training data and decision processes. Most challengingly, it requires acknowledging that no system can be perfectly unbiased and building mechanisms for recognition and correction of bias when it occurs.

The right to understand your computer emerges as a fundamental principle for AI-native systems. This isn't about understanding every technical detail—most people don't understand the physics of transistors in current computers. It's about understanding how decisions that affect you are made, what information systems use, and how to influence outcomes. It's about maintaining human agency in an age of artificial intelligence.

This right manifests in multiple ways. Users should understand what data AI systems collect and how they use it. They should be able to query why certain decisions were made—why an application was given resources, why a suggestion was offered, why access was granted or denied. They should be able to correct misunderstandings and modify behaviors they find problematic. The system should be a comprehensible partner, not an inscrutable oracle.

Implementing this right faces serious challenges. How do you explain decisions emerging from billions of neural network parameters? How do you provide transparency without overwhelming users with complexity? How do you balance the need for understanding with the benefits of sophisticated AI processing? These aren't just interface design challenges but fundamental questions about the relationship between humans and intelligent machines.

Education becomes crucial in this new landscape. Just as widespread literacy was essential for the print age and digital literacy for the computer age, AI literacy becomes essential for the age of intelligent systems. People need to understand not the technical details of neural networks but the nature of probabilistic systems, the possibilities and limitations of AI, and how to maintain agency when working with adaptive systems.

This education can't be limited to formal settings. AI-native operating systems must teach users as they use them, building understanding through interaction. They must reveal their nature gradually, helping users develop intuition about how they work. They must empower users to become not just consumers but partners in the intelligence process.

The next chapter explores the transition period as we move from current systems to AI-native ones. This transition will be neither smooth nor immediate. It will require careful planning, gradual migration, and constant attention to the social implications explored here. The future we're building demands not just new technology but new wisdom in how we deploy it.

CHAPTER 19

Transition Period

The revolution won't happen overnight. There will be no moment when we wake up to find our traditional operating systems replaced by AI-native ones, no instant when the old world ends and the new begins. Instead, we face a transition period likely to span a decade or more—a time of hybrid systems, gradual migrations, and fundamental shifts in how we think about computing. This transition may prove more challenging than the destination itself, requiring us to maintain two paradigms simultaneously while building bridges between them.

History offers lessons about technological transitions. The shift from mainframes to personal computers took nearly two decades. The migration from desktop to mobile computing spanned fifteen years and isn't truly complete. The move to cloud computing continues today, twenty years after it began. Each transition followed patterns we're likely to see repeated: early adopters experimenting with immature technology, hybrid periods where old and new coexist, gradual migration as benefits become clear, and eventual obsolescence of older systems. But the transition to AI-native operating systems presents unique challenges that may make previous shifts seem simple by comparison.

Hybrid architectures will dominate the transition period, blending traditional and AI-native approaches in ways that preserve functionality while enabling innovation. These aren't temporary compromises but sophisticated systems designed to operate in both worlds simultaneously. Imagine an operating system with a traditional kernel managing hardware resources, a compatibility layer running legacy applications, and an AI layer providing intelligent services—all working together seamlessly.

The challenge lies in making these layers truly integrated rather than merely coexistent. When you issue a natural language command, the system must determine whether to route it to AI processing or translate it to traditional system calls. When an application requests resources, the system must decide whether to handle it through predictive AI allocation or traditional scheduling. When data needs storage, the system must choose between semantic embedding and traditional file systems—or somehow use both.

These architectural decisions cascade through every system component. Memory management must handle both deterministic allocations for traditional programs and flexible reservations for AI models. Security systems must protect both static configurations and dynamic learning models. Network stacks must support both packet-based protocols and semantic information exchange. Each component becomes more complex, handling dual paradigms while preparing for eventual convergence.

The user experience during this transition requires particular care. People shouldn't need to consciously switch between "AI mode" and "traditional mode." The system should present a unified interface that intelligently routes requests to appropriate handlers. Natural language commands should work everywhere, even if they're translated to traditional operations behind the scenes. Legacy applications should gain AI capabilities without requiring rewrites. The seams between old and new must be invisible to users even as they're carefully managed by the system.

Migration strategies vary dramatically between individual users and large organizations. For individuals, migration might be as simple as upgrading to a new version that includes AI capabilities, then gradually adopting new features as comfort grows. But for organizations with thousands of custom applications, millions of documents, and complex workflows, migration becomes a multi-year project requiring careful planning and execution.

The data migration challenge alone is staggering. Organizations have accumulated decades of files in hierarchical folder structures. These must be processed to extract semantic meaning, generate embeddings, and establish relationships—all while maintaining accessibility through traditional methods. A financial services firm might have millions of documents that need semantic processing while remaining available for regulatory compliance. A healthcare organization must maintain patient record integrity while enabling AI-powered diagnostics.

Application migration presents different challenges. Some applications can gain AI capabilities through system services—a traditional word processor might suddenly understand natural language formatting commands. Others might need wrapper layers that translate between paradigms. Still others might require complete rewrites to fully leverage AI-native capabilities. Organizations must triage applications, deciding which to enhance, which to replace, and which to maintain as-is.

The most successful migration strategies acknowledge that perfection isn't the goal—progress is. Organizations that attempt complete transitions fail. Those that identify specific pain points and address them with AI-native solutions succeed. A manufacturing company might start by applying predictive maintenance to critical equipment. A retail chain might begin with AI-powered inventory management. Each success builds confidence and expertise for broader adoption.

Risk management during migration becomes

crucial. Traditional systems are well-understood with known failure modes. AI systems introduce new uncertainties. What happens when natural language processing misinterprets a critical command? How do you rollback an AI system that has been learning and adapting? How do you maintain business continuity when core systems are in flux? Smart organizations run parallel systems, maintaining traditional backups while experimenting with AI-native approaches.

Developer ecosystem evolution represents perhaps the most fundamental shift of the transition period. Developers who've spent careers writing deterministic code must learn to work with probabilistic systems. The mental model shifts from defining exact behaviors to guiding intelligent systems. It's like the difference between programming a robot to follow specific paths and training an animal to navigate independently.

New tools and frameworks emerge to support this transition. Integrated development environments (IDEs) gain AI assistants that don't just autocomplete code but understand intent and suggest architectures. Debugging tools evolve from tracing execution paths to visualizing neural network decisions. Testing frameworks must validate not just correctness but appropriateness—does the AI behave reasonably across diverse inputs?

Programming languages themselves evolve to support AI-native development. New constructs emerge for defining probabilistic behaviors, managing context, and coordinating AI agents.

Traditional languages gain libraries and extensions for AI integration. Domain-specific languages appear for particular AI tasks—natural language processing, computer vision, multi-agent coordination. The programming landscape becomes richer but more complex.

The shift in development practices goes beyond tools to fundamental methodologies. Waterfall and even agile approaches assume you can define requirements and verify implementation. But how do you specify requirements for a system that learns? How do you verify behavior that's supposed to adapt? New methodologies emerge that embrace uncertainty, continuous learning, and emergent behavior. Development becomes more like cultivation than construction.

Version control takes on new meaning when code includes trained models. A small code change might require retraining that produces dramatically different behavior. Dependencies include not just libraries but training data, model architectures, and learned parameters. Reproducibility—fundamental to software engineering—becomes challenging when randomness is inherent to the system. New practices emerge for managing this complexity.

Educational requirements for the transition period span multiple audiences with different needs. Current developers need to understand AI concepts without necessarily becoming machine learning experts. They need intuition about how AI systems behave, when to use them, and how to integrate them with traditional code. It's like teaching automotive engineers about electric powertrains—they don't need to understand quantum mechanics of batteries, but they need to know how electric motors differ from combustion engines.

System administrators face their own learning curve. Managing AI-native systems requires understanding new failure modes, performance characteristics, and optimization strategies. They must learn to monitor not just CPU and memory usage but model accuracy and drift. They need to manage not just software updates but model retraining. The role evolves from maintaining static systems to shepherding learning ones.

End users require perhaps the most subtle education. They must develop intuition about probabilistic systems—understanding that responses might vary, that systems learn from interaction, that perfect consistency isn't always desirable. They need mental models for maintaining agency with adaptive systems. Most importantly, they need confidence to engage with systems that might seem unnervingly intelligent.

Educational institutions struggle to keep pace. Computer science curricula built around algorithms and data structures must expand to include machine learning and AI systems. But it's not just about adding AI courses—it's about integrating AI thinking throughout the curriculum. Operating systems courses must cover both traditional and AI-native architectures. Software engineering must include probabilistic systems. Even theoretical computer science must grapple with systems that learn and adapt.

Industry training programs emerge to fill gaps. Major technology companies offer certification programs for AI-native development. Online platforms provide hands-on experience with hybrid systems. Communities of practice form around specific challenges—migrating legacy systems, developing AI agents, managing hybrid architectures. The education happens as much through peer learning as formal instruction.

The transition period also reveals unexpected challenges and opportunities. Legacy systems sometimes gain surprising capabilities when enhanced with AI—old code suddenly understanding new types of inputs. Hybrid architectures enable innovations neither pure traditional nor pure AI systems could achieve. The constraints of supporting both paradigms force clever solutions that advance both.

The next chapter looks beyond the transition to explore what becomes possible in the next decade. When AI-native operating systems mature, when hybrid architectures give way to fully integrated systems, when a generation grows up with intelligent computers as natural as smartphones are today—what new capabilities emerge? The transition is challenging, but the destination justifies the journey.

CHAPTER 20

Next Decade

Standing at the edge of the AI-native operating system revolution, we can see the outline of changes that will transform not just how we compute, but what computing means. The next decade promises developments that push the boundaries of what we consider possible. Brain-computer interfaces are helping paralyzed patients control robotic limbs. Autonomous systems are making decisions without human oversight. AI models are developing capabilities that surprise even their creators. Screens—the windows through which we've viewed the digital world for fifty years—are beginning to seem as quaint as punch cards. These aren't separate trends but converging forces that will shape the second generation of AI-native systems.

The evolution of AI models themselves represents perhaps the most fundamental driver of change. Current large language models, impressive as they are, represent early attempts at creating truly intelligent systems. The next decade will likely see models that don't just process language but truly understand context across multiple modalities —vision, sound, touch, even taste and smell. These won't be separate models awkwardly stitched together but unified architectures that perceive and understand the world more like humans do.

We're already seeing hints of this evolution. Models that can generate images from text descriptions, understand videos, compose music, and write code. But current systems treat these as largely separate capabilities. The next generation will feature deep multimodal integration where understanding flows naturally between different types of information. Describing a scene in words, sketching it visually, humming its soundtrack—all become equivalent ways of communicating with systems that truly understand rather than merely process.

More profoundly, these models are developing what researchers call emergent capabilities—abilities that weren't explicitly programmed or trained but arise from the complex interactions within the neural networks. Models trained on text spontaneously develop internal representations of space, time, and causality. They exhibit reasoning patterns their creators didn't anticipate. As models grow larger and training becomes more sophisticated, we're likely to see emergent capabilities that fundamentally change what AI systems can do.

The architecture of AI systems is evolving

from monolithic models to ecosystems of specialized agents. Instead of trying to create one model that does everything, the next decade will see operating systems coordinating thousands of specialized AI agents, each expert in narrow domains but capable of sophisticated collaboration. These agents won't just share data—they'll share understanding, building collective intelligence that exceeds any individual capability.

This agent-based architecture enables AI systems to evolve continuously without disrupting existing capabilities. New agents can be added for emerging needs. Outdated agents can be retired gracefully. Agents can specialize for individual users or specific contexts. The operating system becomes less like a fixed platform and more like a living ecosystem that grows and adapts over time.

Brain-computer interfaces represent another frontier that's transitioning from research to reality. Current interfaces are limited—detecting general brain activity patterns or allowing simple cursor control. But the trajectory is clear: toward systems that can interpret intentions, emotions, and complex thoughts directly from neural activity. This isn't about reading minds but about creating new channels of communication between human cognition and artificial intelligence.

The implications for operating systems are profound. Instead of translating thoughts into words, then words into commands, brain-computer interfaces could communicate intent directly.

Imagine forming the intention to organize your research and having the system understand not just the task but your preferred organization style, the connections you find meaningful, and the insights you're seeking. The bandwidth of human-computer interaction, constrained for decades by keyboards and screens, could expand by orders of magnitude.

Early applications focus on accessibility—enabling paralyzed users to control computers, helping stroke victims communicate, restoring sensory input for those who've lost it. But as the technology matures and becomes less invasive, it will likely expand to augment healthy users. We might see neural interfaces that enhance memory by connecting to AI systems, accelerate learning by optimizing information presentation for individual brains, or enable new forms of creativity by linking human intuition with AI capability.

The ethical and safety challenges are staggering. How do we ensure security when the interface connects directly to our brains? How do we maintain privacy when thoughts become data? How do we preserve human agency when the boundary between our cognition and AI assistance blurs? These aren't just technical challenges but fundamental questions about human identity and autonomy in an age of intelligent machines.

Autonomous computing systems represent the logical evolution of AI-native operating systems. Current systems, even with AI integration, remain tools that respond to human direction. Autonomous systems would operate independently, pursuing goals, solving problems, and even setting their own objectives within defined parameters. This isn't artificial general intelligence—it's narrow AI with agency, systems that can operate without constant human oversight.

We see early examples in narrow domains. Autonomous vehicles navigate without drivers. Algorithmic trading systems make market decisions in microseconds. Industrial control systems optimize complex processes continuously. But these are isolated instances. The next decade will likely see autonomous capabilities integrated into general-purpose operating systems, creating computers that don't just respond to users but actively work on their behalf.

Imagine a computing environment that doesn't wait for you to assign tasks but identifies opportunities and pursues them. While you sleep, it might analyze patterns in your work, identify potential improvements, and prepare detailed proposals for your review. During your workday, it could handle entire workflows autonomously—not just scheduling meetings but conducting preliminary negotiations, preparing customized materials for each participant, and following up on action items. It becomes less an assistant and more a trusted deputy.

The key to making autonomous systems safe and beneficial lies in alignment—ensuring their goals remain compatible with human values and intentions. This requires new approaches to specifying objectives that capture not just what we want done but why we want it done. We need systems that understand context, values, and consequences, that can make judgment calls aligned with human ethics rather than just optimizing metrics.

The post-screen era might be the most visible change of the next decade. Screens have dominated computing since the first terminals replaced teletype machines. We've made them smaller, larger, and more numerous, but the basic paradigm hasn't changed: information displayed on flat surfaces that we view with our eyes. This constraint has shaped everything about how we interact with computers.

Augmented reality glasses are the most obvious successor, overlaying digital information onto the physical world. But the transformation goes deeper than replacing monitors with head-mounted displays. When computing can appear anywhere in your visual field, the entire world becomes your interface. Information appears where and when it's needed—recipes floating above ingredients, repair instructions overlaying broken devices, navigation cues embedded in the environment itself.

But visual augmentation is just the beginning. Spatial audio can place sounds precisely in three-dimensional space, creating rich information environments that don't require visual attention. Advanced haptics provide touch sensations for virtual objects, making digital information tangible. Even smell and taste interfaces, currently experimental, might mature within the decade.

Computing becomes truly embodied, engaging all our senses rather than primarily our eyes.

Perhaps the most profound aspect of the post-screen era is ambient computing—intelligence embedded in the environment rather than confined to devices. Every surface could become computational through smart materials and projection. Furniture adapts to your needs. Rooms reconfigure based on activities. The environment itself becomes responsive and intelligent. You don't interact with a computer; you inhabit an intelligent space.

This ambient intelligence requires AI-native operating systems that can coordinate countless devices, maintain context across environments, and present information in whatever form is most appropriate. The operating system doesn't run on a device—it runs on the environment itself, creating coherent experiences as users move through physical and digital spaces.

The social integration of AI-native systems will transform how we work, learn, and connect. Education becomes truly personalized, with AI tutors that understand each student's learning style, pace, and interests. Work becomes more creative as AI handles routine tasks and humans focus on innovation and judgment. Social connections deepen as AI helps bridge communication gaps and cultural differences.

We're likely to see the emergence of AI-mediated communities where collective intelligence solves problems beyond any individual's capability.

Imagine citizen scientists collaborating through AI systems that translate between different expertise levels, aggregate insights, and identify patterns across contributions. Or creative communities where AI helps artists build on each other's work, musicians jam across continents, and writers craft stories together despite speaking different languages.

The next decade will also bring challenges we're only beginning to understand. How do we maintain human agency when AI systems become so capable? How do we ensure equity when advanced interfaces require sophisticated hardware? How do we preserve privacy when computing is ambient and pervasive? How do we maintain meaning and purpose when machines can do so much of what once defined human work?

These questions don't have easy answers, but they're not reasons to slow progress. Instead, they're design challenges that must be addressed as we build these systems. The operating systems of the next decade must be designed not just for capability but for human flourishing. They must amplify human potential while preserving human agency. They must connect us while respecting our autonomy. They must be powerful while remaining comprehensible.

The convergence of these trends—evolving AI models, brain-computer interfaces, autonomous systems, and ambient computing—points toward a future where intelligence isn't artificial or natural but simply present. Where the boundary between thought and action, between intention and accomplishment, becomes gossamer-thin. Where computers don't just process our commands but understand our goals and help achieve them in ways we hadn't imagined.

We're not heading toward a future where machines replace humans but one where human and machine capabilities merge into something greater than either alone. The AI-native operating systems we're building today are the foundation for this synthesis—creating environments where human creativity, judgment, and values are amplified by artificial intelligence that understands, supports, and enhances rather than replaces.

The next decade will be extraordinary, challenging, and transformative. We're not just building operating systems—we're designing the cognitive infrastructure for humanity's future.

GLOSSARY

AI-Native Operating System: An operating system designed from the ground up with artificial intelligence as its core architecture, rather than traditional deterministic computing models.

Anytime Algorithm: An algorithm that can provide a valid solution even if interrupted before completion, with quality improving given more computation time.

AUTOSAR Adaptive: AUTomotive Open System ARchitecture standard for adaptive platforms in vehicles, supporting dynamic software updates and AI workloads.

Behavioral Consistency: In distributed AI systems, ensuring that collective actions align despite individual variations in processing or decision-making.

Capability-Based Security: A security model where access rights are conveyed through unforgeable tokens (capabilities) rather than access control lists.

Confidential Computing: Technology that protects data during processing by performing computation in hardware-based secure enclaves.

Context Window: In large language models, the amount of text or information that can be processed and maintained during a single interaction.

Differential Privacy: A system for sharing information about datasets while withholding information about specific individuals within the dataset.

Edge AI: Artificial intelligence processing performed on local devices at the network edge rather than in centralized cloud servers.

Embeddings: High-dimensional numerical representations that capture the semantic meaning of content (text, images, etc.) in vector space.

Federated Learning: A machine learning technique that trains algorithms across distributed devices or servers while keeping data localized.

GPU-Aware Scheduling: Resource scheduling that understands and optimizes for graphics processing unit characteristics and requirements.

Homomorphic Encryption: Encryption that allows computation on encrypted data without decrypting it first.

Intel TDX: Intel Trust Domain Extensions, hardware technology for creating isolated, encrypted execution environments.

Knowledge Distillation: Training smaller, more efficient neural networks to mimic the behavior of larger, more complex models.

Kubeflow: An open-source platform for deploying and managing machine learning workflows on Kubernetes.

Large Language Model (LLM): AI models trained on vast amounts of text data capable of understanding and generating human-like text.

Microkernel: An operating system architecture that runs most services in user space rather than kernel space, providing better isolation and security.

Multi-Agent System: A system composed of multiple interacting intelligent agents, each with specialized capabilities.

Neural Engine/NPU: Specialized hardware designed specifically for accelerating neural network computations.

ONNX Runtime: A cross-platform inference engine for deploying machine learning models trained in various frameworks.

OPEA: Open Platform for Enterprise AI, a Linux Foundation project establishing standards for enterprise AI systems.

Predictive Scheduling: Scheduling algorithms that anticipate future resource needs based on learned patterns rather than reacting to current demands.

Probabilistic Kernel: A theoretical OS kernel that manages uncertainty, context, and meaning rather than just deterministic resources.

Quantization: Reducing the precision of neural network weights (e.g., from 32-bit to 8-bit) to decrease model size and increase efficiency.

Secure Multi-Party Computation: Cryptographic methods enabling parties to jointly compute functions over their inputs while keeping those inputs private.

seL4: A formally verified microkernel proven to implement its specification correctly.

Semantic File System: A storage system organized by meaning and relationships rather than hierarchical directory structures.

Software 1.0/2.0/3.0: Terms describing the evolution from traditional programming (1.0) through machine learning (2.0) to natural language-driven computing (3.0).

TinyML: Machine learning techniques and technologies designed for resource-constrained microcontrollers and IoT devices.

Vector Database: A database optimized for storing and retrieving high-dimensional embeddings for semantic search.

Zero-Knowledge Proof: A cryptographic method where one party can prove knowledge of information without revealing the information itself.

REFERENCES

Operating System Architecture and Microkernels

Heiser, G., & Elphinstone, K. (2016). "L4 Microkernels: The Lessons from 20 Years of Research and Deployment." *ACM Transactions on Computer Systems*, 34(1), 1-29.

Klein, G., Elphinstone, K., Heiser, G., Andronick, J., Cock, D., Derrin, P., ... & Winwood, S. (2009). "seL4: Formal Verification of an OS Kernel." *Proceedings of the ACM SIGOPS 22nd Symposium on Operating Systems Principles*, 207-220.

Liedtke, J. (1995). "On Micro-Kernel Construction." *Proceedings of the 15th ACM Symposium on Operating System Principles*, 237-250.

Tanenbaum, A. S., & Woodhull, A. S. (2006). *Operating Systems Design and Implementation* (3rd ed.). Pearson Prentice Hall.

Large Language Models and AI Foundations

Brown, T., Mann, B., Ryder, N., Subbiah, M., Kaplan, J. D., Dhariwal, P., ... & Amodei, D. (2020). "Language Models are Few-Shot Learners." *Advances in Neural Information Processing Systems*, 33, 1877-1901.

Devlin, J., Chang, M. W., Lee, K., & Toutanova, K. (2019). "BERT: Pre-training of Deep Bidirectional

Transformers for Language Understanding." *Proceedings of NAACL-HLT*, 4171-4186.

Vaswani, A., Shazeer, N., Parmar, N., Uszkoreit, J., Jones, L., Gomez, A. N., ... & Polosukhin, I. (2017). "Attention Is All You Need." *Advances in Neural Information Processing Systems*, 30.

Wei, J., Tay, Y., Bommasani, R., Raffel, C., Zoph, B., Borgeaud, S., ... & Fedus, W. (2022). "Emergent Abilities of Large Language Models." *Transactions on Machine Learning Research*.

Neural Processing Units and AI Hardware

Chen, Y., Luo, T., Liu, S., Zhang, S., He, L., Wang, J., ... & Chen, T. (2014). "DaDianNao: A Machine-Learning Supercomputer." *Proceedings of the 47th Annual IEEE/ACM International Symposium on Microarchitecture*, 609-622.

Jouppi, N. P., Young, C., Patil, N., Patterson, D., Agrawal, G., Bajwa, R., ... & Yoon, D. H. (2017). "In-Datacenter Performance Analysis of a Tensor Processing Unit." *Proceedings of the 44th Annual International Symposium on Computer Architecture*, 1-12.

Reuther, A., Michaleas, P., Jones, M., Gadepally, V., Samsi, S., & Kepner, J. (2019). "Survey and Benchmarking of Machine Learning Accelerators." *2019 IEEE High Performance Extreme Computing Conference*, 1-9.

Confidential Computing and Privacy-Preserving AI

Costan, V., & Devadas, S. (2016). "Intel SGX Explained." *IACR Cryptology ePrint Archive*, 2016(86),

1-118.

Dwork, C., & Roth, A. (2014). "The Algorithmic Foundations of Differential Privacy." *Foundations and Trends in Theoretical Computer Science*, 9(3-4), 211-407.

Kairouz, P., McMahan, H. B., Avent, B., Bellet, A., Bennis, M., Bhagoji, A. N., ... & Zhao, S. (2021). "Advances and Open Problems in Federated Learning." *Foundations and Trends in Machine Learning*, 14(1-2), 1-210.

Li, T., Sahu, A. K., Talwalkar, A., & Smith, V. (2020). "Federated Learning: Challenges, Methods, and Future Directions." *IEEE Signal Processing Magazine*, 37(3), 50-60.

Edge Computing and TinyML

Banbury, C., Reddi, V. J., Lam, M., Fu, W., Fazel, A., Holleman, J., ... & Whatmough, P. (2021). "Benchmarking TinyML Systems: Challenges and Direction." *arXiv preprint arXiv:2003.04821*.

Shi, W., Cao, J., Zhang, Q., Li, Y., & Xu, L. (2016). "Edge Computing: Vision and Challenges." *IEEE Internet of Things Journal*, 3(5), 637-646.

Warden, P., & Situnayake, D. (2019). *TinyML: Machine Learning with TensorFlow Lite on Arduino and Ultra-Low-Power Microcontrollers*. O'Reilly Media.

Container Orchestration and Enterprise AI

Burns, B., Grant, B., Oppenheimer, D., Brewer, E., & Wilkes, J. (2016). "Borg, Omega, and Kubernetes." *ACM Queue*, 14(1), 70-93.

Hindman, B., Konwinski, A., Zaharia, M., Ghodsi, A., Joseph, A. D., Katz, R., ... & Stoica, I.

(2011). "Mesos: A Platform for Fine-Grained Resource Sharing in the Data Center." *Proceedings of the 8th USENIX Symposium on Networked Systems Design and Implementation*, 295-308.

Semantic Storage and Vector Databases

Johnson, J., Douze, M., & Jégou, H. (2019). "Billion-Scale Similarity Search with GPUs." *IEEE Transactions on Big Data*, 7(3), 535-547.

Malkov, Y. A., & Yashunin, D. A. (2018). "Efficient and Robust Approximate Nearest Neighbor Search Using Hierarchical Navigable Small World Graphs." *IEEE Transactions on Pattern Analysis and Machine Intelligence*, 42(4), 824-836.

AI Safety and Alignment

Amodei, D., Olah, C., Steinhardt, J., Christiano, P., Schulman, J., & Mané, D. (2016). "Concrete Problems in AI Safety." *arXiv preprint arXiv:1606.06565*.

Russell, S. (2019). *Human Compatible: Artificial Intelligence and the Problem of Control*. Viking Press.

Industry Reports and Standards

AUTOSAR Consortium. (2022). "AUTOSAR Adaptive Platform Specification." Release R22-11.

Linux Foundation. (2023). "Open Platform for Enterprise AI (OPEA) Technical Charter." Version 1.0.

NVIDIA Corporation. (2023). "NVIDIA DRIVE AGX Platform Documentation." Developer Documentation Series.

National Institute of Standards and Technology. (2023). "AI Risk Management Framework." NIST AI 100-1.

Historical Perspectives

Karpathy, A. (2017). "Software 2.0." Medium. [Blog post describing the concept of Software 2.0]

Patterson, D. A., & Hennessy, J. L. (2021). *Computer Architecture: A Quantitative Approach* (6th ed.). Morgan Kaufmann.

Ritchie, D. M., & Thompson, K. (1974). "The UNIX Time-Sharing System." *Communications of the ACM*, 17(7), 365-375.

Emerging Technologies

Abadi, M., Barham, P., Chen, J., Chen, Z., Davis, A., Dean, J., ... & Zheng, X. (2016). "TensorFlow: A System for Large-Scale Machine Learning." *Proceedings of the 12th USENIX Symposium on Operating Systems Design and Implementation*, 265-283.

Paszke, A., Gross, S., Massa, F., Lerer, A., Bradbury, J., Chanan, G., ... & Chintala, S. (2019). "PyTorch: An Imperative Style, High-Performance Deep Learning Library." *Advances in Neural Information Processing Systems*, 32.

Printed in Dunstable, United Kingdom